CONFESSIONS
OF A KEPT WOMAN
A FAITH JOURNEY TO PEACE, PURPOSE, AND ABUNDANT LIVING

CONFESSIONS
OF A KEPT WOMAN
A FAITH JOURNEY TO PEACE, PURPOSE, AND ABUNDANT LIVING

BARBARA HARRIS CURTIS

Back2Back Books
Houston, Texas

CONFESSIONS OF A KEPT WOMAN

A Faith Journey to Peace, Purpose, and Abundant Living

Cover Design: D-Mars, Houston, Texas

Cover Photo: Images to Remember, Houston, Texas

Text Composition: Barry K. Henry-Grafikally Speaking, Houston, Texas

DEDICATION

I dedicate *Confessions of Kept Woman* to my beloved mother,
Geneva Harris.

Mom,

I am truly blessed to have a loving, caring, and
praying mother. I thank God for you!

Thank you for the many sacrifices you have made for me.
Thank you for your encouraging words that have inspired me
along this journey of faith.

Thank you also for your loving chastisement that
helped me to stay on the right path.

Most of all, thank you for introducing me to the Keeper of your
soul – the One I now call my very own – our Lord and Savior,
Jesus Christ.

I love you, mom,
Barbara

Many mothers have done well,
but you out shine them all. I rise up and bless you.
(Proverbs 31:29, author's paraphrase)

IN LOVING MEMORY OF

My grandmother, Pearline Curl
and
My aunt, Elean Phlegm

Acknowledgments

So many people prayed for me, encouraged me, and assisted me in the achievement of this dream. Though I cannot list every one of your names here, please know that your acts of kindness and support are forever embedded in my heart.

Special thanks:

To my wonderful husband Larry, for covering me in prayer and showering me with love.

To my sister Cathy Howard, for planting the first financial seed for this vision.

To my prayer partners – Rosalind Caldwell, Felicia Cheek, Carolyn Clansy, Cynthia Curry, Wonderland Hudson, Angela Jones, Donna Joseph, Petite McCowan, Diane Milburn, Danni Pruitt, Honornell Sandling, and Pamela Smith – for being faithful friends who always "have my back."

To my "unofficial" project team – Donna Bennett, Vanessa Blackstone, Renee Branson, Jane Cartwright, Tongela Clark, Darnecia Claybon, Siobhan Johnson, Danita King, Shawn Morgan, Tisha Traylor, Earnestine Wagner, Sharon Warren, and Carolyn Yarbro – for your assistance and support.

To God be the glory!

CONTENTS

INTRODUCTION

*W*riting a book is an enormous undertaking, and this one has been a long time coming. I thought that I would never make it past the title page, but here I am embarking upon a journey that is unmapped but divinely directed...uncertain and yet absolutely sure.

I would like to begin by sharing with you all of the wonderful things that this book is. Then, I will tell you what it is not.

This book is an answer to prayer. It is a God-given vision written to transform the lives of all of those who read it and take it seriously.

This book is for those of you who desire change in your lives but are not quite sure where to start. It is for those who have tried the advice of the experts, with no success. Your shelves may be lined with enough books and tapes to open your own resale store, but you still have no "proof of your purchases" beyond the receipts. If you are like most, you've probably never gotten past the first few days (or hours) of your self-help plans.

This book is for those of you who yearn for a closer walk with God, a more confident sense of self, and healthier relationships with others. This book is for those of you who believe that there is more to life than what you are experiencing right now. It is for those of you who want it all – not all that the world says you should have, should be, and should do but all that God has promised and purposed for you –spiritually, emotionally, financially, socially, and physically.

In short, this book is for those of you who are ready to tap into the secrets of living the abundant life. I don't claim to have achieved perfection in my own life, but like Paul in Philippians 3:12-14, I press on toward the goal. Experience has taught me that it is a lot easier to "press" using the right training and tools. No serious athlete would enter a race, a marathon, a fight, a game, or any other demonstration of endurance without the proper training and tools. So if you're serious about pressing toward the goal in this "race" called life, this book is for you.

Confessions of a Kept Woman is not about me. My testimony is woven throughout the book for the purpose of illustration, but the foundation of each chapter and each topic is the Word of God. The confessions at the end of each chapter are God's Word – His promises that speak to our pains, passions, and situations. The Bible says that both death and life are in the power of the tongue (Proverbs 18:21). I am convinced that many of us are not experiencing the abundant life God has promised because we are constantly speaking death into our circumstances. For example, we are confessing that we are broke, rather than empowered to obtain wealth. We are confessing that we are sick, instead of healed by His stripes. We are confessing the defeat of depression, not the joy of the Lord.

We must learn to think and say what God thinks and says about our situations. His Word is powerful, and it produces extraordinary results in our lives. The tragedy is that many of us do not know His Word. Therefore, we have little or no knowledge of His promises and our privileges as His children.

You are about to take a faith journey, and Scripture tells us that faith comes by hearing, and hearing by the Word of God (Romans 10:17). Therefore, it is imperative that your path is paved with the Word of God. If you do not already have a good study Bible, I encourage you to purchase one. I don't want you to just take what I say and run with it. I want you to read and search the Scriptures for yourself. This will also help you to grow in your love for, knowledge of, and relationship with our Lord and Savior, Jesus Christ.

Throughout this book, I will use different translations of Scripture, but I will frequently refer to the New Living Translation. This translation literally transformed my understanding of and appreciation for the Word of God. I have recommended this version to hundreds of others who largely agree that it opens doors of understanding that were previously blocked by the language barriers of older translations, such as the King James Version.

I highly recommend that you consider investing in the New Living Translation. However, please note that I am not affiliated with the publisher, nor am I marketing the product. My intent is simply to introduce you to a tool that may increase your level of biblical understanding. I trust that you will carefully and prayerfully select the translation that best suits your needs.

Now, it is time to begin the journey of your life. I hope that you share my excitement and expectation for all that God is going to do for you and through you as you step into a new season of peace, purpose, and abundance.

Let's go!

CHAPTER ONE

❊

HE'S A KEEPER

Give yourself to God; you can be sure
He will take care of what is His.

— Patti LaBelle —

The title of this book came to me in a very unexpected and supernatural way. It was during a season in my life when everything seemed to be spinning out of control. I was confronted with challenges in just about every area of my life, including my ministry, my health, my finances, and my relationships. I tried everything that I knew to get back on track, but nothing seemed to work. Thankfully, I was spiritually grounded enough to know that I needed the wisdom, peace, and strength that only God could provide. I began to seek the Lord and His guidance like I had never done before, praying and searching His Word for answers to the overwhelming problems in my life.

One Sunday, after my regular worship service, I got in my car and cried out loud, "Lord, I need to hear from you today. Why have you been silent?" My exact steps after that are a little fuzzy to me now, but I remember deciding to stop at a friend's church in the area. I had promised to visit, and this was a perfect time.

Arriving a little late, I entered into one of the most powerful praise and worship services that I have ever experienced. We sang several soul-stirring songs, but those that spoke to my spirit the most were those that described God as a "Keeper": "Jesus Keep Me Near the Cross", "He Just Keeps On Blessing Me", and "Just Another Day That the Lord Has Kept Me."

I can't tell you what the pastor's message was that morning, but through the praise and worship, God spoke directly to me. The scripture that He whispered to me was Isaiah 26:3. Deep down in my spirit, I clearly heard His voice: "I will keep in perfect peace all who trust in Me, whose thoughts are fixed on Me."

This passage was not new to me. I distinctly remember my first encounter with it. I am sure that I had read it many times before, but during this memorable experience, it came as a personal word from God, assigned especially to me. My grandmother, who was very dear to me, had just passed away, and I was struggling with excruciating grief. The enemy had also managed to add guilt to the equation (all of the should haves, would haves, and could haves).

Additionally, I harbored deep resentment toward the church that my family and I attended for what I perceived to be their lack of concern and compassion for my grandmother during her lengthy illness and hospital stay. If that wasn't enough emotional turmoil, I had also just come to the agonizing but long overdue conclusion that the relationship I was involved in was neither healthy nor ordained by God.

The grief, pain, anger, disappointment, guilt, and loneliness were overwhelming. At this very dark time in my life, God used my cousin Ruby – unbeknownst to her – to initiate the process of my healing. She simply gave me a small figurine in the shape of a dove with the inscription: "You will keep him in perfect peace, whose mind is stayed on You, because he trusts in You" (KJV).

The praise and worship that Sunday morning had the same effect as the little figurine. Throughout the service, I reflected on the countless times that God had brought me through seemingly impossible situations. I remembered the times that He had been faithful to His promises in my life, and I realized that there are many times in life when His promises are all that we have to "hold on to." God revealed to me on that morning that I am a "kept woman."

> THERE ARE MANY TIMES IN LIFE WHEN HIS PROMISES ARE ALL THAT WE HAVE TO "HOLD ON TO."

Careful study of Isaiah 26:3 further revealed the meaning of my "kept woman" revelation. In order to gain a better understanding of the passage, I defined the key words in the text.

> You will keep in perfect peace all who trust in You,
> whose thoughts are fixed on You!

The word "peace" comes from the Greek word "eirene" which means wholeness, completeness, and tranquility in the soul that is unaffected by outward circumstances or pressures.

The dictionary provides the following definitions for the word "keep:" (1) to be faithful to, (2) to watch over and defend, (3) to take care of, and (4) to preserve or maintain in a good, fitting, or orderly condition.[1]

In the Greek, the word "mind" depicts the central place from which a person perceives, comprehends, and controls his or her environment.

The word "fixed" means not subject to change or fluctuation.[2]

Given these definitions, a practical translation of Isaiah 26:3 could read:

> *If we keep our minds and our thoughts focused on God,*
> *then He will faithfully take care of us and keep us in a*
> *state of wholeness and calm that cannot be affected*
> *by the circumstances surrounding us.*

When I look back, God has been a faithful "Keeper" in my life. He has taken good and loving care of me. My grandmother and I were so close that many who knew of our bond wondered how or even if I would be emotionally able to handle her death. To be perfectly honest with you, there were many days when even I wasn't sure, but I made it. He kept me!

Furthermore, circumstances in my life have demanded that I be very independent. Since a very early age, I have had to be the caretaker, the strong one, the glue that held everything together. Marrying later in life than I ever expected (at age 44) added to this state of independence. I was sincerely one of the most "satisfied" single women that I knew. I had learned to enjoy life and God's blessings in my single state. Yet, there were times when I – like most honest, independent women – longed for someone to "take care of me." I can still remember struggling with financial challenges, wishing that I had someone in my life to help pay the bills. I remember attending the funerals of loved ones, wishing that I had someone to comfort me. I remember being sick and shut in, wishing that I had someone to "come and see about me." Through it all, God *kept* me.

He kept me from falling apart when everything
around me seemed unstable.

He kept me from losing my mind when worry and anxiety
seemed to follow me closer than goodness and mercy.

He kept me from giving up when going
on seemed impossible.

He kept me company when loneliness seemed to
be my only companion.

He kept me safe when my enemies attempted
to destroy me.

He kept me focused when circumstances
would have otherwise distracted me.

He kept me encouraged when despair
encamped all around me.

God's indescribable, unexplainable, perfect peace kept
my soul anchored during the inescapable storms of life.

This "kept woman" revelation has been life-changing for me. Through it, I have discovered God's prescription for a life of peace, purpose, and abundance. I have learned to stand firmly on the Word of God...refusing to allow circumstances and situations to control me...keeping my mind fixed and focused on Him and His promises...trusting Him to keep, guard, and care for me...allowing His Word to direct my thoughts, my conversations, my actions, and ultimately my destiny.

I pray that this journey will deposit the same transforming truths into your life.

THOUGHT QUESTIONS

1. Reread Isaiah 26:3. In your own words, what does God promise us in this passage?

_____

_____

_____

_____

_____

_____

2. Reflect for a few moments on one of the most difficult experiences in which God "kept" you. Summarize it here.

_____

_____

_____

_____

_____

_____

_____

3. To what or to whom do you most often turn for comfort? Why?

_____

_____

_____

_____

_____

_____

_____

4. Which outward circumstances or pressures most often upset your peace of mind?

_____

_____

_____

_____

_____

_____

_____

5. What difference would it make in your life if your "mind stayed fixed on Him?"

_____

_____

_____

_____

_____

_____

_____

6. What did God reveal to you through this chapter?

_____

_____

_____

_____

_____

_____

_____

What will you do with these revelations? Which changes will you make? Which actions will you take?

_____

_____

_____

_____

_____

_____

_____

_____

_____

_____

_____

_____

_____

_____

_____

CONFESSIONS

I keep my mind and my thoughts focused on God and His Word. I place my trust in Him. He faithfully provides for every one of my needs, and He keeps me in a state of wholeness and calm that cannot be affected by the circumstances surrounding me.
(Isaiah 26:3 and Philippians 4:19)

I constantly fill my mind with and think about things that are true, good, lovely, pure, and right. I don't dwell on negative, unholy, or unpleasant thoughts.
(Philippians 4:8)

I am a blessed woman because I trust in the Lord. I place all of my hope and confidence in Him. I am like a strong tree planted along a riverbank, with roots that reach deep into the water. I am not bothered by the dry seasons or adverse conditions that surround me. My leaves stay healthy and green, and I continuously flourish.
(Jeremiah 17:7-8)

I keep God's Word in my heart. I do not forget what He has taught me. His words give me a long, satisfying, and peaceful life.
(Proverbs 3:1)

The Lord is my Keeper.
He stands beside me as a protective shade.
(Psalm 121:5)

I am not troubled or afraid because my heavenly Father has given me a wonderful gift – peace of mind and heart. And the peace He gives isn't like the peace the world gives. It isn't conditional – here today and gone tomorrow.
(John 14:27)

Which point from this chapter speaks directly to one of your personal situations? Search God's Word for relevant promises and write a faith confession concerning the matter.

CHAPTER TWO

YOU POSSESS
WHAT YOU CONFESS

Scientific research is conclusive that your self-talk
has a direct bearing on your performance. In reality, the most
influential person who will talk to you all day is you,
so you should be very careful about what you say to "you."

– Zig Ziglar –

will never forget the day I discovered the power of words. I, like many others, had never given much thought to my conversations. I remember my former pastor Kirbyjon Caldwell asking the congregation, "Why do you all go around trying to catch colds?" At first, I thought, "Pastor, have you lost your mind?" as I watched him running around the pulpit, grasping at the air as if trying to catch hold of something. (Pastor Caldwell is one of the most demonstrative and effective speakers that I know.) Then, it clicked. He was so right. How many times had I detected a scratchy throat, stuffy head, or other cold symptom and proclaimed, "I'm trying to catch a cold"? As I sat chuckling at the examples Pastor Caldwell used to illustrate how we speak negative circumstances into our lives, I began to seriously consider my internal and external conversations. I began to list some of the destructive declarations that I had either made or heard others make...

I am sick and tired of ...

I'll never...

I can't...

I'm too (fat, skinny, stupid, far behind, tall, short)...

My hair is a mess.

He/she makes me sick.

Nobody cares about me.

The more I try to get ahead, the farther behind I get.

I'll never pay off all of these bills.

It looks like I'll never get married.

My husband/wife will never change.

We have the worst kids on the block.

I could never afford...

I don't have what it takes to...

I never have enough money.

I can't get anywhere on time.

I keep making the same mistakes.

I just washed my car; it'll probably rain.

My children are driving me crazy.

I can't get any rest around here.

I could never...

This is a dead-end job.

Trouble just seems to follow me.

I hope you are getting the picture. We have what we say. Too often, our words are self-destructive tools that unconsciously sabotage our success. The Bible tells us that death and life are in the power of the tongue (Proverbs 18:21). Our words can literally create or destroy. This creative power dates as far back as the beginning of time. The first chapter of the Book of Genesis – the creation story – magnificently illustrates the power of the spoken word. Each time God spoke, He released creative power.

> TOO OFTEN, OUR WORDS ARE SELF-DESTRUCTIVE TOOLS THAT UNCONSCIOUSLY SABOTAGE OUR SUCCESS.

> In the beginning God created the heavens and the earth.
> The earth was empty, a formless mass cloaked in darkness.
> And the Spirit of God was hovering over its surface.
> Then God said, "Let there be light," and there was light...
> Genesis 1:1-3

God has given us the same creative power and authority. We can literally speak life or death into our situations. When our words align themselves with God's Word, we see His blessings and promises manifested in our lives. Unfortunately, too many of our words align more with the enemy's plan – to kill, steal, and destroy – than with God's plan to give us abundant life.

You are probably familiar with the following expression: "Sticks and stones may break my bones, but words will never hurt me." Now, we all know that this statement is untrue. Words are powerful! All of us can recall hurts, pains, and deep wounds caused by their careless use.

When was the last time you listened to what you are saying? What are you saying about your circumstances, your potential, and your future? You may be surprised, as I was, to realize that many of the problems in your life originate from your own mouth. If your conversations and self-talk are filled with negative, critical, pessimistic words, then you are literally committing "conversational suicide." You are killing your self-esteem, your potential, your dreams, your relationships, and other aspects of your life. If this sounds like you, stop it!

God has done a great work in you and has a wonderful plan for your life. His Word is filled with truths about who you are, what you possess, and what is available to you. Begin today to come into agreement with His Word. We must believe that we *are who He says we are; we can do what He says we can do; and we can have what He says we can have.* Align your mouth with the Truth. Silence the enemy's lies. Put your words to work for you, rather than against you.

> IF YOUR CONVERSATIONS AND SELF-TALK ARE FILLED WITH NEGATIVE, CRITICAL, PESSIMISTIC WORDS, THEN YOU ARE LITERALLY COMMITTING "CONVERSATIONAL SUICIDE."

In Hebrews 10:23 (NKJV), we are instructed to "hold fast the confession of our hope without wavering, for He who promised is faithful." Regardless of what is going on around us, only faith-filled confessions, rooted and grounded in the Word of God, should come out of our mouths.

In his book *Sparkling Gems from the Greek*, author Rick Renner explains, *"The word 'profession' used in Hebrews 10:23 (or 'confession,' as it is translated in other scriptures), from the Greek word homologia, is not the picture of a person who simply repeats what someone else says. This is an individual who has gotten God's Word into his heart and who has come into agreement or alignment with what God says. This person sees a matter like God sees it; hears it like God hears it; feels it like God feels it. Now his heart and God's heart are so unified on the issue that their hearts are nearly beating in syncopation with each other. Thus, when the believer opens his mouth to 'confess' God's Word, his confession is no longer powerless empty chatter; instead, it comes from a very deep place of conviction inside his heart."*

It took me a while to fully grasp this revelation. At first I thought, "Well, I'm just speaking the truth. This is how I really feel; this is how I actually look; or this is just the way it is." I would hear others making faith confessions and think they were a fanatical bunch of liars. I didn't realize that I had not fully comprehended the Truth, and therefore, I, not they, was speaking, believing, and living the enemy's lies. I had to learn to speak and to rely on the Truth instead of the "facts." In some cases, the facts were clear. My bank account was low. My weight was up. My job was undesirable. But none of these facts were in alignment with the Truth – God's Word.

> ...Your Word is Truth.
> John 17:17 (AMP)

I had a choice to make. I could keep talking about what I had, or I could start confessing what I'm promised. I could keep my focus and my words on the problems, or I could switch my focus and my confessions to God's Word. I chose to change my focus and clean up my conversations. No longer would I speak self-defeating, counterproductive words.

This newfound practice did not come easy. My bad habit was indeed hard to break. As I became more aware of my words, I was amazed at how much I used them to my detriment. At times, in disbelief over the words that I had just spoken, I had to ask myself, "Where did that come from?" The Holy Spirit would then remind me:

> ...For whatever is in your heart determines what you say.
> Matthew 12:34

In other words, whatever is inside of us will come out of us. Therefore, we have to guard our minds and hearts by carefully screening what we see, hear, read, and otherwise allow into our

WHATEVER IS INSIDE OF US WILL COME OUT OF US. THEREFORE, WE HAVE TO GUARD OUR MINDS AND HEARTS BY CAREFULLY SCREENING WHAT WE SEE, HEAR, READ, AND OTHERWISE ALLOW INTO OUR MINDS.

minds. We cannot constantly consume negative images and messages without experiencing negative effects on our thoughts, our words, and ultimately our lives. On the other hand, if our inbound images and messages are positive, the effects will be positive.

For years, I witnessed my mother suffer from one ailment after the other. After discovering the power of words, I began to examine my mother's conversations, most of which pertained to her physical condition. Most of her confessions were similar to these:

"I'm sick."

"This medicine is not working."

"My doctors don't know what they're doing."

God revealed to me that my mother's thoughts and words were literally "making her sick." Yes, she did have some legitimate health issues, but her confessions were making matters worse. I realized that I had to get her to change her thoughts and her words regarding her health. I will never forget the look she gave me when I explained to her the power of words and that I believed she was speaking some of her ailments into existence. I'm certain that her immediate thought was, "Help me, Lord. Not only am I sick, but now my child has lost her mind!"

I convinced her to just give it a try...to just try to speak positive words about her health...to try to find something positive about her physical condition and to focus on that everyday. Furthermore, I began to consciously direct and redirect the flow of our conversations. Initially, these changes were a stretch for both of us. At times, our conversations would make both of us chuckle. I would ask, "How are you doing today, mom?" and she would reply, "I'm just going to *say* that I'm fine." "Praise the Lord!" I would respond. After a while, we began to see a real change. My mother's physical condition took a turn for the better!

Having always been a woman of great faith, my mother now realized that her thoughts and words regarding her health had to be faith-filled. By putting "life" back into her mouth, she literally put "life" back into her years.

> Pay attention, my child, to what I say. Listen carefully.
> Don't lose sight of my words. Let them penetrate deep within
> your heart, for they bring life and radiant health to anyone
> who discovers their meaning.
>
> Proverbs 4:20-22

Through this and other miraculous experiences in my own life, I have learned to take God at His Word. Whenever I'm faced with any decision or circumstance, I immediately search the Scriptures for God's Word regarding the situation. I then began to meditate on and speak His Word. Time after time, I've seen the Word of God move mountains in my life.

> For assuredly, I say to you, whoever says to this mountain,
> "Be removed and be cast into the sea," and does not doubt
> in his heart, but believes that those things he says will be done,
> he will have whatever he says.
>
> Mark 11:23 (NKJV)

I have seen God's Word move mountains of fear, doubt, lack, sickness, anxiety, worry, strife, and confusion. Some of these mountains seemed insurmountable and many took time to move. I had to learn to stand on His Word and to not waver during the times when nothing seemed to be happening. It wasn't always easy

YOU POSSESS WHAT YOU CONFESS

to confess and believe the Truth when the "facts" were clear.

It's not easy to speak health and long life
when the x-ray shows a spot.

It's not easy to speak abundance
when your checking account is overdrawn.

It's not easy to speak peace when you feel like
you're about to lose your mind.

It's not easy to speak forgiveness
when you've been betrayed by someone you trusted.

It's not easy to speak patience
when your dream has been delayed...again.

Consider the story of Abraham and Sarah. God promised to make Abraham the father of many nations, but the facts were not on Abraham's side.

> When God promised Abraham that he would become
> the father of many nations, Abraham believed him. God
> had also said, "Your descendants will be as numerous as
> the stars," even though such a promise seemed utterly
> impossible! And Abraham's faith did not weaken, even
> though he knew that he was too old to be a father at the age
> of one hundred and that Sarah, his wife, had never been
> able to have children. Abraham never wavered in believing
> God's promise. In fact, his faith grew stronger, and in this
> he brought glory to God. He was absolutely convinced
> that God was able to do anything he promised.
>
> Romans 4:18-21

Abraham's example is good for all of us. Even in seemingly impossible times, we must hold on to God's promises. We must stand firmly on the uncompromising truth of His Word and allow it to become rooted in our hearts and thoughts. When His Word becomes rooted in us, we can draw peace and strength from it during difficult times. When His Word becomes rooted in us, our thoughts and words become more promise-driven than problem-driven. His Word rooted in us, makes it more natural for us to "call those things that do not exist as though they did" (Romans 4:17).

Resolve today to stop focusing on your problems. Nursing and rehearsing them do not solve them. Begin replacing your problem-driven confessions with promise-driven ones. Here are some examples.

PROBLEM-DRIVEN	PROMISE-DRIVEN
My company is laying people off; I may be next.	God's favor surrounds me like a shield, and all of my needs are met.
My children are getting on my nerves.	My children are blessings from God, and they add so much joy to my home.
My enemies are out to get me.	I am more than a conqueror in Christ, and no weapon that is formed against me will prosper.
I'm depressed.	I have the peace of God that surpasses all understanding, and His peace guards my heart and mind.
I'm broke.	My God supplies all of my needs, and I want for nothing.
I can't...	I can do all things through Christ who strengthens me.
I'm so ashamed.	God does not condemn me, and neither do I condemn myself.
I should've...	I will not dwell on the past; rather, I forget those things that lie behind me, and I press forward.

As you begin to change your thoughts and words, you will also begin to see changes in your circumstances. These changes may not be instantaneous, but if you're consistent with your confessions, you'll experience the peace and strength needed to endure until you actually possess what you confess.

THOUGHT QUESTIONS

1. Do you spend time meditating on and memorizing Scripture? If yes, describe your routine.

_____

_____

_____

_____

_____

_____

_____

_____

If not, brainstorm three practical ways that you can begin to fill your mind with the Word.

_____

_____

_____

_____

_____

_____

_____

_____

_____

2. Check the words below that describe your frequent self-talk:

☐ Positive   ☐ Negative   ☐ Fearful

☐ Faith-filled   ☐ Problem-driven   ☐ Purpose-driven

☐ Thankful   ☐ Ungrateful   ☐ Pessimistic

☐ Optimistic   ☐ Stressful   ☐ Peaceful

Are you sabotaging your success by thinking thoughts or speaking words that are not in alignment with God's Word? If so, explain.

_____

_____

_____

_____

_____

_____

_____

_____

3. Have you ever noticed your mood shifting after watching a particular television show or after listening to certain types of music? What did this experience teach you?

_____

_____

_____

_____

_____

_____

_____

4. When was the last time that you were surprised by something negative you said? What does this tell you about the condition of your heart at that time?

_____

_____

_____

_____

_____

_____

_____

5. What did God reveal to you through this chapter?

_____

_____

_____

_____

_____

_____

_____

What will you do with these revelations? Which changes will you make? Which actions will you take?

_____

_____

_____

_____

_____

_____

_____

_____

_____

CONFESSIONS

The Word of God is a lamp for my feet,
providing the light that I need to see my way.
(Psalm 119:105)

I desire to live a life that is long and good; therefore,
I am careful regarding my words. I do not tell lies.
(Psalm 34:12-13)

I have faith in God. He has given my words creative power.
Whatever I believe in my heart and speak
from my mouth – without doubt – I can have.
(Mark 11:23)

I am a good woman, with a good heart;
therefore, I speak good words.
(Matthew 12:35)

The words of Christ dwell richly in my heart, making me wise.
I use His words to teach, encourage, and counsel others. I
sing songs of praise to Him. I represent Christ in all that I do
and say, giving thanks to God through Him.
(Colossians 3:16-17)

The Lord has given me words of wisdom. Each morning, He
awakens me and teaches me to understand His will.
(Isaiah 50:4)

I will bless the Lord at all times.
His praise will always be in my mouth.
(Psalm 34:1)

I abide in the Lord, and His Word abides in me; therefore, I
can ask God for anything, and I will receive it.
(John 15:7)

Which point from this chapter speaks directly to one of your personal situations? Search God's Word for relevant promises and write a faith confession concerning the matter.

_____

_____

_____

_____

_____

_____

_____

_____

_____

_____

_____

_____

_____

_____

_____

_____

_____

CHAPTER THREE

WHO DO YOU THINK YOU ARE?

You cannot consistently act in a manner
inconsistent with the way you see yourself...
If you don't believe that you have potential,
you will never try to reach it.

— JOHN MAXWELL —

*O*f all the opinions formed about you, the most
important is the one formed in your own mind. The
Bible says, "as a woman thinks in her heart, so is she" (Proverbs
23:7a, paraphrased). Self-image is at the core of everything
we aspire to, everything we accomplish, and everything we
accept. An unhealthy self-image is more damaging to dreams,
relationships, careers, and marriages than any outside influences
or circumstances.

The familiar story of the prodigal son is told in Luke 15:11-32.
You've probably heard it preached many times, so I won't expound
on the details. Verses 16 and 17 alone are packed with powerful
lessons.

> The boy became so hungry that even the pods
> he was feeding the pigs looked good to him.
> But no one gave him anything.

> When he finally came to his senses, he said to himself,
> At home even the hired men have food enough to spare,
> and here I am dying of hunger!..."

Even without knowing the story in its entirety, one can deduce from these verses that the young man was living at a level far beneath that of his inherited position. He was starving to death while even the servants "at home" enjoyed more than enough food to eat.

Picture the young man for a moment, wallowing miserably in a literal pigpen. Suddenly, he experiences an awakening that causes him to talk to himself, saying, "Wait a minute. What am I doing here with these pigs? I can do better than this. Even the servants at my father's house live better than I'm living now."

Does this passage echo a chapter in your own life? Have you ever been there, wallowing miserably in the pigpen of life? Or maybe this describes your present state. Maybe your marriage, relationship, financial situation, home, job, or life has become a pigpen. You're at a place where you can no longer bear the "mess." You're hungry for more. You deserve better.

I, too, at different junctions along the journey, have found myself in life's pigpens – dead-end situations far off the path of my divine destiny. Thank God, my final destination was not the pigpen, and neither is yours. God has a wonderful plan for you.

> "For I know the plans I have for you," says the Lord.
> "They are plans for good and not for disaster,
> to give you a future and a hope."

JEREMIAH 29:11

So, how do you move from here to there? How do you make the turn? How do you change directions when the journey seems to be reaching a dead-end?

The compelling quote by John Maxwell at the beginning of this chapter warrants repeating:

You cannot consistently act in a manner
inconsistent with the way you see yourself...
If you don't believe that you have potential,
you will never try to reach it.

What you think and believe about yourself directly influences everything that you do. If you desire positive changes in your life, then you have to see yourself in a manner consistent with those changes. Like the young man in the story, if you're going to change your circumstances, you first have to change your thoughts concerning them. When the young man finally came to his senses, he realized that his lifestyle did not match his heritage. Before this awakening, he had begun to accept and even desire a life that was never meant for him. I would even venture to say that he thought he deserved the pigpen. He had reached the mental place where he could no longer see himself outside of his situation.

> IF YOU DESIRE POSITIVE CHANGES IN YOUR LIFE, THEN YOU HAVE TO SEE YOURSELF IN A MANNER CONSISTENT WITH THOSE CHANGES

Meditate for a few minutes on the following quote by Elmer Towns:

Much of what we do in life is a response to the way we see ourselves.
You can't achieve what you can't conceive!
It is good to develop the ability to see ourselves
as we really are, but more importantly,
to develop the ability to see ourselves as we want to be.

Assuredly, self-concept plays a critical role in the journey to peace, purpose, and abundance. Therefore, it is imperative that we see ourselves the way God sees us. His thoughts and ways are far above and beyond anything we can imagine (Isaiah 55:8). Therefore, we must renew our minds to His way of thinking.

> Don't copy the behavior and customs of this world,
> but let God transform you into a new person by changing
> the way you think. Then you will know what God
> wants you to do, and you will know how good and
> pleasing and perfect his will really is.

ROMANS 12:2

I have been blessed by frequent encounters with levels of living far beyond that of my present financial means. On one such occasion, a colleague and I were invited to visit the home of a wealthy couple. During a breathtaking and impressive tour (the place was massive and exquisitely decorated), my colleague shook her head in awe and commented, "I just can't see myself living in a place like this." After pausing for a moment and trying to determine from which "inner" place her comment originated, I suddenly became aware of the root issue. Sympathetically, I thought to myself, "Based upon your own confession and lack of vision, you will probably never live in a place like this." In other words, if you cannot formulate a mental picture of an existence different from your present state of being, it will be difficult, if not impossible, for you to reach that place.

Unlike my friend, I had no problem visualizing myself in a home of equal or greater magnificence. As I toured each room, I began to mentally redecorate with the furnishings and color schemes of my own taste, and not an ounce of jealousy or envy entered my thoughts. On the contrary, I sincerely complimented my hosts and thanked God for their peaceful and palatial home. I also silently confessed, based on Acts 10:34, "God, You are no respecter of persons; You show no partiality. What You've done for them, You can do for me."

47

This thought process began early in my life. I can vividly remember, as a young girl, visiting the homes of my Girl Scout troop leaders and others whom the Lord strategically placed in my life. These homes, though modest (I now realize), were quite impressive to a little girl from the "hood." I can remember thinking, "When I grow up, I'm going to have a big house like this."

I am eternally grateful to my mother who contributed greatly to the development of my self-image and outlook on life. When I was very young, she introduced me to my Heavenly Father and my royal heritage (1 Peter 2:9). This knowledge of who and Whose I am is the foundation upon which my thoughts and dreams are built.

This same God-confidence is available to you. The Bible instructs us not to think more highly of ourselves than we should, but rather to have a Christ-centered self-concept (Romans 12:3). Once you've established a firm, biblical concept of who and Whose you are, everything that you do – and the way that you do it – will be different. The way that you approach and manage relationships, challenges, and opportunities will reflect your new self-worth, which will come from your relationship with God and your understanding of His Word. Others will also begin to treat you differently and to regard you with higher esteem, not because their opinions of you have changed, but because yours has.

Most of us know people who have not attained a lot in terms of education, wealth, or material possessions; and yet some of these same individuals live fulfilled lives and command a great deal of respect. On the other hand, there are those who possess all of the outward signs of success and yet have no inner value. We see this every day in the lives of celebrity figures with whom many of us dream of trading places, without having a true understanding of the whole picture. We peek into their lives from a distance and ask ourselves, "How could a woman so beautiful keep finding herself in destructive, abusive relationships?" "How could a person with that much money be depressed and addicted to drugs?" "How could a person who 'has it all' be so miserable?" The answer is simple: true joy, peace, and fulfillment are found in our self-worth, not our net worth. As a matter of fact, money, power, and prestige are dangerous and often short-lived in the hands of a person with an unhealthy self-image.

> TRUE JOY, PEACE, AND FULFILLMENT ARE FOUND IN OUR SELF-WORTH, NOT OUR NET WORTH

Looking back at the young man in Luke 15:16-17, we see a person who went from riches to rags, having wasted all of his money on wild living (verse 13). I assume that he wasted a lot of money trying to impress people, trying to buy friendships and relationships, and trying to build himself up in the eyes of his associates. Consequently, it didn't take long for his net worth to plunge to the depths of his self-worth. And sadly, none of the people he had "wined and dined" would give him anything when he hit rock bottom (verse 16). When he finally came to his senses, he refused to accept his circumstances and began the process of recovery. He realized that he was not a pig and refused to live like one.

So, who do you think you are? I hope you realize that you are God's child, His heir, and a joint heir with Christ (Romans 8:17). If you don't know this, I pray that you will "come to your senses," correct your vision, and begin to see yourself as your Heavenly Father does. Spend time in His Word, meditating on and confessing His thoughts concerning your value. The Bible says that God created you in His image (Genesis 1:26) and declared that you are excellent in every way (1:31). Beginning in Genesis, gather the scriptural truths that you need to journey beyond your self-imposed limitations and into your divine destiny.

Don't allow anything, any thought, or anyone to hold you back. It doesn't matter how low you've sunk or how far you've drifted, God's forgiveness and His grace are available to you. He's standing – like any loving father – with open arms ready to receive you. You are His child. Don't ever forget the fact that this relationship has its privileges.

God gave me the following poem to remind me of and empower me with some of His thoughts concerning His daughters. I share it with you in the hope that it will become a part of your daily confessions, thereby resulting in the manifestations of His promises in your life.

I AM

Who does she think she is?
That's really the question behind the stare.
I wish that they would ask outright
So I could boldly declare...

I am of royal priesthood – my Father is Christ, the King
I'm created in His image, fearfully and wonderfully made
He knew of His wonderful plans for me
Before even the sun and the moon were laid

Strength and dignity are my clothing
A crown of righteousness adorns my head
My Father's promises to me include health and wealth
And I receive every word He said

Please don't misinterpret my God-confidence
It's not conceit or arrogance
The Bible says that I am a joint heir with Christ
And I choose to claim my inheritance

I give God the praise and the glory
Through Him, I can do all things
I am exceedingly and abundantly blessed
I am of royal priesthood, a daughter of Christ, the King

THOUGHT QUESTIONS

1. Think back to your earliest recollections of self. List five words that describe your feelings about yourself at that time in your life.

_____

_____

_____

_____

_____

_____

Was your self-image positive or negative at that time? Which internal or external factors helped to shape this self-image?

_____

_____

_____

_____

_____

_____

2. Think about one of your most significant relationships (romantic, friendly, or professional). Describe the way you're treated by this person.

_____

_____

_____

_____

_____

_____

How might your self-image be influencing this treatment?

_____

_____

_____

_____

_____

_____

_____

_____

_____

3. Have you ever wished that you were more like another person? If so, search the Word of God for scriptures that help you to see the value of your own uniqueness and list them here.

_____

_____

_____

_____

_____

_____

_____

_____

_____

_____

4. At this season in your life, is there any area that feels like a "pigpen"? Are you living beneath your potential and settling for less than God's best? If, so describe that situation.

_____

_____

_____

_____

_____

_____

_____

_____

_____

_____

_____

_____

_____

Which steps can you begin taking today to move in the direction of your God-ordained destiny?

_____

_____

_____

_____

_____

_____

_____

_____

_____

5. What did God reveal to you through this chapter?

_____

_____

_____

_____

_____

_____

_____

_____

What will you do with these revelations? Which changes will you make? Which actions will you take?

_____

_____

_____

_____

_____

_____

_____

_____

CONFESSIONS

All of God's works are marvelous, and I am one of His masterpieces. I am confident of this.

(Psalm 139:14)

I give all praise, glory, and honor to my heavenly Father, who has blessed me with every spiritual blessing in Christ. I am His beloved daughter. I was on His mind before I was ever conceived. Before He created the world, He chose me to be holy and blameless in His sight. It is by His grace that I am saved through faith in Jesus Christ. I could never have earned such a wonderful gift. I am His careful design, recreated in Christ Jesus with the ability to fulfill the plan and reach the destiny that He ordained for me long ago.

(Ephesians 1:3-6, 2: 8-10)

I am obedient to God's voice. I am blessed everywhere I go and in everything that I do. I obey God's Word and walk in His ways. People see that I am chosen and called by God, and they stand in awe of me. I am a lender, not a borrower. I am the head and not the tail; above only, and not beneath.

(Deuteronomy 28:1-13)

I am Christ's ambassador and the righteousness of God.

(2 Corinthians 5:20,21)

I am God's own child, an heir through Christ. I have full rights to all of His promises. His Holy Spirit resides in me. I know Him personally, and I will never be a slave to false gods.

(Galatians 4:5-9)

Which point from this chapter speaks directly to one of your personal situations? Search God's Word for relevant promises and write a faith confession concerning the matter.

CHAPTER FOUR

REALITY CHECK

*If you have never been bound, you have
no idea how good it feels to be free!*

— BISHOP T. D. JAKES —

*O*ne thing that I have learned along the journey to peace,
purpose, and abundance is that in order to get to the
place where God wants you to be, you first have to determine
where you are – spiritually, emotionally, financially, physically, and
relationally.

The first question asked by God in Scripture is, "Where are
you?" In Genesis 3:8, the Lord confronts Adam with this thought
provoking inquiry. The Lord's question is not for His benefit, but
for Adam's. God in His omniscience knew Adam's precise location
and condition. The purpose of the question was to provoke Adam's
self-examination.

It disturbs me when I think about the many facades, excuses,
and lies that people live behind. This is a trick of the enemy,
for which too many of us have fallen. Nothing has to be "real."
We have been taught that we can just "fake it until we make it."
However, the truth is that you can only "fake it" and "hide it" for so
long. Sooner or later, as in the situation with Adam and Eve, the
"real deal" will be revealed.

God has an awesome plan and purpose for your life, but you have to take a "real" look at where you are before you can begin to map out the directions to your divine destiny. The goal of this chapter is to help you face the truth regarding circumstances and situations in your life. I must warn you that the truth can sometimes be painful in the beginning, but it will ultimately set you free (John 8:32).

> THE TRUTH CAN SOMETIMES BE PAINFUL IN THE BEGINNING, BUT IT WILL ULTIMATELY SET YOU FREE.

The Bible teaches us that satan, our enemy, is the father of all lies (John 8:44). Two of his most powerful, demonic offspring are delusion and denial. These lethal states of mind are assigned to destroy our self-esteem, our dreams, our relationships, our potential, and ultimately our lives. The two either collaboratively or independently weave a web of hopelessness in our minds that captures and strangles our peace and wholeness.

THE DEMON OF DELUSION

Delusion is defined as: (1) something that is falsely believed or (2) a persistent false psychotic belief regarding the self or persons or objects outside of self.[1]

Someone once said, "There are three you's – the you that you think you are, the you that others think you are, and the real you." Have you ever asked yourself the question, "Who am I?" If not, now is a good time to do so. Take a good, honest look at yourself. Are you comfortable with the person that you see? What do you believe about yourself? What do you say about yourself? What do family members, friends, co-workers, and others believe and say about you? How were these beliefs developed?

We are all born with a healthy sense of self, but at a very early age, we begin to form opinions (positive and negative) about ourselves based on words, behaviors, and expectations directed at us by others.

Think back to your earliest memories of your self-image. What did you think about yourself as a child? I'll assist you with this question by sharing some of my own memories.

I am the sixth of eight children (five older brothers, one younger brother, and one younger sister). I grew up in a very loving but very "tough" environment. There was no time or tolerance in our household for weakness. At a very early age, I realized that I had to be tough. I was constantly teased by my brothers about my weight, big head, and dark skin. Needless to say, as a child, I never thought of myself as beautiful. I compensated for my looks by excelling in school and became known as the "smart one," not the "cute one" that I really wanted to be. This early image of self followed me through life like a stalker. At times, I was aware of its presence and effect; at others, I was not. I now realize that the weight battle, the shopping obsession, the drive to excel, the "tough girl" image, and the perfectionism that I have struggled with over the years all stem, in one way or another, from these opinions of self formed long ago. The demon of delusion began feeding me lies as soon as I was old enough to start digesting them.

I thank God that He has not allowed the demon of delusion to destroy me. However, the battle never really ceases. That stalker from my past still appears uninvited and does his best to "break and enter" into my thoughts, but I have learned to recognize him. Futhermore, I have developed a self-defense strategy to protect me from his subtle and blatant attacks, and I strongly encourage you to do the same.

Take note of the satanic static going on in your mind. The Bible says that as a man or woman thinks, so is he or she (Proverbs 23:7a). This is a scary statement for some of us because our perceptions of ourselves are so negative. However, the good news is that our minds can be renewed. This renewal can also lead to positive life changes.

One such transformation began in my life when I decided that my full figure, head size, and skin tone are "all good" because God says they are. This new attitude required, and still requires, some work. I have had to face some facts and respond accordingly. For instance, my weight at one point in my journey became more than I was able to bear physically and emotionally. At that point, I had two choices: (1) keep eating, whining, and complaining, or (2) lose the weight. So I made up my mind to lose the weight. In six months, I lost sixty pounds and gained a new lease on life. The pounds had been shackles tied to each of my feet, literally weighing me down and preventing me from running, walking, or even crawling towards my destiny.

This is not a book on weight loss, but I will tell you this – the pounds start in your head before they ever reach your hips. The battle of the bulge begins in your mind. I have read many books and heard many testimonies on the weight issue, and it all boils down to the same truth: "No diet or exercise plan will work if you do not have a made-up mind."

I thank God that He has taught me to love and respect my body, which is His temple. I now realize that God created me, and He does not create junk. I am comfortable with the fact that I could never be a stuntwoman for Halle Berry or Julia Roberts; that is not my calling. However, I am still fearfully and wonderfully made, and marvelous are His works (Psalm 139:14).

Furthermore, our minds, not our eyes, are our windows to the world. Changing the way we think about things, situations, other people, and ourselves can literally open up a whole new world to us. This window analogy reminds me of my former home and the home of a friend. My friend's home has a magnificent view. Every window in her home looks out on acres of exotic landscaping, plush green grass, flowing fountains, and other breathtaking scenery. The windows of my former home, on the other hand, opened up to the backs and sides of my neighbors' homes, yielding a dull view of bricks and mortar from most angles. My home and my friend's home were both actually surrounded by beauty. However, the view from my windows could appear lifeless if I allowed it. I had to make up my mind that I would not allow the brick walls to block my blessings. That home was a blessing from God. It was a place where I found true peace, happiness, and refuge. I had to learn to focus on the flowers and shrubs planted around the walls, the majestic trees towering over the walls, and the bright morning sun or the beautiful evening stars divinely positioned above and beyond the walls – not the walls themselves.

What is obstructing your view today? Has the demon of delusion constructed brick walls in your life that are successfully blocking your blessings and keeping you from realizing and experiencing the beauty all around you?

WE CANNOT KEEP THOUGHTS FROM KNOCKING ON THE DOORS OF OUR MINDS, BUT WE CAN DETERMINE WHETHER OR NOT TO ALLOW THEM ENTRY.

Decide today to reject every deceptive thought – about yourself, about others, and about circumstances – that the demon of delusion hurls your way. The Bible instructs us to surrender our thoughts to God (2 Corinthians 10:5). We accomplish this by filling our minds with His thoughts, found in His Word. Additionally, we must continuously guard our thoughts. We must be aware of what we allow to enter our minds. I know that many of our thoughts are involuntary. They seem to come out of nowhere, but we are still in control of them. We cannot keep thoughts from knocking on the doors of our minds, but we can determine whether or not to allow them entry. If our minds are already filled with God's Word, this leaves no room for delusive guests.

THE DEMON OF DENIAL
Denial is defined as a psychological defense mechanism in which confrontation with a personal problem or with reality is avoided by denying the existence of the problem or reality; refusal to admit the truth or reality.[2]

If you are going to begin to experience the peaceful, purposeful, and abundant life that God has promised, you must destroy the demon of denial. You must come face to face with the lies that have clothed your situations and circumstances. Layer by layer, you must strip them off in order to find peace with the naked truth that lies beneath.

As women, many of us can fully relate to this analogy. No matter how many girdles, control-top garments, and figure-flattering styles we use to "cover up," we must, sooner or later, face our bodies. If we are overweight and choose to deny and cover up the extra pounds, then we will never experience improved physical and emotional health.

This brings to mind one of my friends who maintained a size six figure throughout college and the first few years of womanhood. However, at some point during her early thirties, the once size six figure blossomed into a size 12. Though the size 12 was flattering and proportionate to her height and shape, she refused to accept the fact that her size six days were over. She spent years in denial, refusing to purchase clothing in her true size and consequently compromising her appearance with tight-fitting attire.

Ultimately, through "loving" truth expressed by well-meaning friends and serious self-examination, my friend realized that she was in denial. This breakthrough resulted in her eventual weight loss, commitment to an exercise regimen, and development of a healthy self-image.

Like my friend, many of us have areas in our lives that need serious examination. God has a way of revealing these areas to us through His Word, the Holy Spirit, and other people. Unfortunately, we often turn a deaf ear to these revelations or deny their validity. African-American heroine Harriett Tubman said it best: "I've freed hundreds of slaves and would have freed hundreds more if they had just known they were slaves" (paraphrased). The journey to freedom from any situation begins with the first step – realizing and admitting that you are in bondage.

> THE JOURNEY TO FREEDOM FROM ANY SITUATION BEGINS WITH THE FIRST STEP – REALIZING AND ADMITTING THAT YOU ARE IN BONDAGE.

Breaking free from any area of bondage is a process. Whether your bondage is physical, financial, relational, emotional, or spiritual, Jesus came to set you free (Luke 4:18). I offer no quick fixes or instant releases. You did not become bound overnight, and you most likely will not break free overnight. I do not deny the power of God to work instantaneous miracles in any situation, but I have most often witnessed Him work through a process.

You can begin this process by asking yourself a simple question – "How am I doing?" This will lead to serious and honest self-examination.

> Examine and test and evaluate your own selves to see whether you are holding to your faith and showing the proper fruits of it.
>
> 2 CORINTHIANS 13:5a (AMP)

Beginning on page 69 are several questions to get you started on the road to discovery. Meditate on Psalm 139 printed below, and then prayerfully begin to answer the questions. Record your answers in a journal or notebook. (I recommend that you keep one of these close at hand while reading this book.) I repeat – record your answers. Do not just think about your responses – write them down. Putting your answers on paper will help you to see your thoughts more clearly.

Psalm 139

O Lord you have examined my heart
and know everything about me.

You know when I sit down or stand up.
You know my every thought when far away.

You chart the path ahead of me
and tell me where to stop and rest.
Every moment you know where I am.

You know what I am going to say
even before I say it, Lord.

You both precede and follow me.
You place your hand of blessing on my head.

Such knowledge is too wonderful for me,
too great for me to know!

I can never escape from your spirit!
I can never get away from your presence!

If I go up to heaven, you are there; if I go down to the
place of the dead, you are there.

If I ride the wings of the morning,
if I dwell by the farthest oceans,

even there your hand will guide me,
and your strength will support me.

I could ask the darkness to hide me
and the light around me to become night

but even in darkness I cannot hide from you.
To you the night shines as bright as day.
Darkness and light are both alike to you.

You made all the delicate, inner parts of my body
and knit me together in my mother's womb.

Thank you for making me so wonderfully complex!
Your workmanship is marvelous and how well I know it.

You watched me as I was being formed in utter seclusion,
as I was woven together in the dark of the womb.

You saw me before I was born.
Every day of my life was recorded in your book.
Every moment was laid out before a single day had passed.

How precious are your thoughts about me, O God!
They are innumerable!

I can't even count them; they outnumber the grains of sand!
And when I wake up in the morning,
you are still with me!

O God, if only you would destroy the wicked!
Get out of my life, you murderers!

They blaspheme you; your enemies take your name in vain.

O Lord, shouldn't I hate those who hate you?
Shouldn't I despise those who resist you?

Yes, I hate them with complete hatred,
for your enemies are my enemies.

Search me O God, and know my heart;
test me and know my thoughts.

Point out anything in me that offends you,
and lead me along the path of everlasting life.

SELF-EXAMINATION
QUESTIONS

How are you doing...

spiritually?

- How would you describe your relationship with God?
- How often do you pray? Do you enjoy your prayer time or consider it obligatory?
- How often do you read/study God's Word?
- Are you comfortable sharing your faith with others?
- Are you an active member of a church?

physically?

- Do you maintain a balanced, healthy diet?
- How often do you exercise?
- Are you overweight/underweight?
- Do you have any habits that jeopardize your health (such as smoking, drugs, or alcoholism)?
- When was your last physical examination?

emotionally?

- Describe your current state of mind.
- Do you struggle with feelings of depression or anxiety?
- Would your friends describe you as a happy person? If not, why?
- Are most of your thoughts about yourself positive or negative?

financially?

- Are you living from paycheck to paycheck?
- Do you have savings and retirement accounts? In the event of the loss of your present income, how long could you maintain your current lifestyle on your savings?
- Are you in credit card debt? If so, how much?
- Do you tithe?

relationally?

- Do you have a close friend/prayer partner?
- If married, describe your relationship with your spouse.
- If single, are you at peace in this season of your life, or are you wrestling with loneliness and/or your biological clock?
- Do you spend quality time with family members and friends?
- Do others enjoy being around you?

Now that you have recorded your responses, reread Psalm 139 and ask the Lord to convict and instruct you in areas where improvement is needed. Please do not rush through or skip this exercise. Spend some time in prayer (talking to God) and meditation (allowing Him to speak to you through His Word and the Holy Spirit). Like Adam in Genesis 3:8, these questions are for your benefit, not God's. God knows everything about you. He knows your strengths, weaknesses, successes, and failures. Do not condemn yourself if your responses indicate a need for improvement in some or even most of the areas. Remember, life is a journey, not a destination. None of us are "there," but you are now in a great place. Now that you know how you are doing, you are properly positioned to do better.

THOUGHT QUESTIONS

1. When one area of our lives is unhealthy or out of order, it can negatively impact other areas. Considering the self-examination questions that you answered earlier in this chapter, which area of your life may be negatively affecting other areas?

_____

_____

_____

_____

_____

_____

_____

2. Are you "faking it" in any area(s) of your life?

_____

_____

_____

_____

_____

_____

3. Which truths have you discovered in God's Word but have not yet begun to live out in you own life?

_____

_____

_____

_____

_____

_____

_____

4. How do you think God would describe you?

_____

_____

_____

_____

_____

_____

_____

_____

_____

5. Do you feel God moving you out of the bondage of the enemy's lies and into the freedom of His truths in any area of your life? What's holding you back? What do you need to break free?

_____

_____

_____

_____

_____

_____

_____

6. What did God reveal to you through this chapter?

_____

_____

_____

_____

_____

_____

_____

What will you do with these revelations? Which changes will you make? Which actions will you take?

_____

_____

_____

_____

_____

_____

_____

_____

_____

_____

_____

_____

_____

_____

_____

CONFESSIONS

I am a true disciple of Christ. I live according to His Word.
His Word is the Truth in my life, and it has set me free from
every snare of the enemy.
(John 8:31-32)

I do not rely on my own power to wage war against the
enemy. I use God's Word and prayer to knock down the
enemy's strongholds. I tear down every thought, every
argument, and every idea that attempt to position themselves
above the truth of God. I do not allow my thoughts to hold me
captive; rather, I surrender them to Christ.
(2 Corinthians 10:3-5)

The Lord helps me to understand the meaning of His
commandments. I cling to His Word. He keeps me from lying
to myself by giving me the privilege of knowing His Truth.
(Psalm 119:27-31)

The Lord God is my Father. I listen gladly to His words.
I refuse to listen to satan, the father of lies.
(John 8:44)

God's words are sweet to my taste; they are sweeter than
honey. His commandments give me understanding.
I love His Word and hate every false way of life.
(Psalm 119:103-104)

Which point from this chapter speaks directly to one of your personal situations? Search God's Word for relevant promises and write a faith confession concerning the matter.

_____

_____

_____

_____

_____

_____

_____

_____

_____

_____

_____

_____

_____

_____

_____

_____

_____

_____

_____

CHAPTER FIVE

HOW TO GET YOUR GROOVE BACK

—

THE RIGHT WAY

I spent a lot of unhappy days because I started thinking about all the wrong things the minute I awoke each morning...I remember when the Lord spoke to me during one of my pity parties. He said, "Joyce, you can be pitiful or you can be powerful, but you cannot be both."

— JOYCE MEYER —

ost of you have seen or heard about the book and subsequent movie *How Stella Got Her Groove Back*. For those who have not, its main character, Stella, is a 40-year-old, single, professional woman who appears to have it all but has lost her *groove*. Stella is bored, discontented, and longing for fulfillment. She and her best friend Delilah take a vacation trip to Jamaica, looking for relaxation and revival. While in Jamaica, Stella meets and falls in love with a younger man (a 20-year-old) who helps her "get her *groove* back."

Shortly after the release of the book and movie, many single women purchased tickets, packed their bags, and *flew* to the islands, looking for love, fulfillment, and fun. Sadly, many discovered that the *groove* found on these excursions usually lasted about as long as the flight home.

After many conversations with numerous female friends and associates about this *groove* craze, I found myself trying to determine the object of everyone's search. I wanted to be sure that I fully understood what my *groove* was before I set out to discover or recover it. First, I looked up "groove" in the dictionary, which contained the following definitions: (1) an enjoyable or exciting experience and (2) to enjoy oneself intensely.[1] I've since formed my own definition: your *groove* is that condition or situation that brings you joy, excitement, pleasure, and fulfillment. Finding your *groove* is being at a place in life where you are pleased with your state of being.

Have you ever lost some or all of your *groove*, resulting in feelings of discontentment and emptiness? I have been there and found myself thinking, "Lord, there has to be more to life than this." Furthermore, as a single woman, I found myself, on many occasions, longing for the joy and excitement that I was certain I could find in a relationship.

I thank the Lord for speaking to me through His Word, encouraging me, and assuring me of His promises during those discontented times in my life. I would like to share with you some simple yet important keys that have helped me and will help you get your *groove* back – the right way. This way will produce lasting results and will not cost you a plane ticket to Jamaica.

The biblical example God gave me for living a full and satisfied life is found in the Book of Ruth. This often-taught book tells the story of two women, Ruth and Naomi. Some characterize it as a beautiful love story, referring to the marriage that takes place between Ruth and Boaz. Others describe it as a portrait of friendship, highlighting the loyal relationship between Ruth and Naomi. Still others view *Ruth* as a story of redemption, depicting Boaz as a type of Christ, our true Redeemer. The Book of Ruth offers all three of these messages and more.

The first chapter introduces us to three widows: Ruth, Naomi, and Orpah. The opening verses present a picture of their grief, despair, and destitution. Thankfully, the story does not end there, at least not for Ruth and Naomi. (Orpah's destiny is not shared with us; all we know is that she chose a different path.) In the midst of their trials, Ruth and Naomi held on to three things that contributed to the return of their *groove*: faith, friendship, and a focus on the future. Like these women, if we are going to experience the joy and fulfillment that God promises, **we must journey by faith, with the support of family and friends, and with our focus on the future.**

BY FAITH

I, like Ruth and Naomi, have found that life has a way of throwing some devastating blows...blows that leave you stumbling or completely knocked off of your feet. I have also found faith to be a vital component in the process of recovery. Whether making a comeback from financial, emotional, relational, or other setbacks, faith has consistently been the rope that has held and supported me until I have been able to steady my feet. It has also been the guiding hand to push me back into the battles of life with renewed strength and determination.

FAITH IS REACHING BEYOND THE PRESENT CIRCUMSTANCES IN YOUR LIFE AND GRABBING HOLD OF GOD'S PROMISES REGARDING THEM.

What is faith? The Bible says that faith is "the confident assurance that what we hope for is going to happen. It is the evidence of things we cannot yet see" (Hebrews 11:1). Along the journey to peace, purpose, and abundant living, we must walk by faith, not by sight (2 Corinthians 5:7). We will not always be able to see our breakthroughs in the natural, but by faith we can believe that they are taking place. Faith is seeing yourself well when the doctor says the lump is malignant. Faith is seeing your marriage as healthy when your husband won't talk to you. Faith is seeing yourself promoted when your manager appears to be sabotaging you. Faith is seeing yourself as spiritually mature when you're not certain whether Jeremiah was a prophet or a disciple. Faith is reaching beyond the present circumstances in your life and grabbing hold of God's promises regarding them. The Word of God is filled with His promises, and our ability to possess them is directly tied to our capacity to receive them by faith.

By faith, Noah built the ark without any sign of rain.

By faith, Abraham left all that was known to him and obediently set out on a journey to the unknown.

If you're ever going to get your groove back, you must – by faith – begin to pursue the joy and peace that God has promised you. Possession, however, requires action on your part. The Bible says that faith without works is dead (James 2:20). Decide today to be happy, to enjoy life, and to love yourself. Stop hosting perpetual pity parties. I too have attended more of these events than I would like to admit. Some have actually been therapeutic, but the tendency is to stay far too long. If you must, go ahead, close the blinds, get your cry out, scream, and holler, but put a timer on it. As with any event, a pity party should have a start and a stop time.

DECIDE TODAY TO BE HAPPY, TO ENJOY LIFE, AND TO LOVE YOURSELF.

I have learned that one night is about all I need to get back on the road to recovery. Not that my situation or mood has changed by dawn, but by daybreak, I've made up my mind that I will not allow the situation or mood to hold me hostage for another day.

I have learned to encourage myself (1 Samuel 30:6), and you must do the same. Do you remember the nursery rhyme "Little Sally Walker"? I love the verse *Rise, Sally, rise...wipe your weeping eyes!* Note that the verse does not mention anyone being there to help Sally to her feet or to wipe away her tears. Sally had to do this for herself, and there will be times when you will have to do the same. The good news is that although no one may be there for you in the natural, God never leaves you or forsakes you (Hebrews 13:5). I *know* what I'm talking about. I have been bound to the bed by disappointments, broken relationships, betrayals, and grief. I have had bruises and wounds so deep that healing seemed impossible. Yet, in each of these situations, my faith proved to be exactly what I needed to nurse me back to life.

IT IS IMPERATIVE THAT WE READ, MEDITATE ON, AND LIVE BY THE WORD OF GOD.

This fire of faith is stirred up in several ways. The Bible says that our faith comes by hearing the Word of God (Romans 10:17). Therefore, it is imperative that we read, meditate on, and live by the Word. Saturate yourself in the Word of God. Turn off all negative messages and allow only His Word to pervade your thoughts.

I remember times when I have felt the loneliness and isolation of a broken relationship. Before I discovered the power of God's Word, my tendency was to host a pity party and wallow in the lyrics of some sad love song. Now, I know better. A Luther Vandross CD is definitely not what you need when "there's no one there to hold you tight." God's Word, on the contrary, is truly medicine for the soul. Make sure that your CD collection includes some *quality* Gospel music. (I emphasize *quality* because there is more to music than the beat. What message

DON'T OVERLOOK THE POWER OF CHURCH ATTENDANCE IN DEVELOPING YOUR FAITH AND RESTORING YOUR SOUL.

is being conveyed? Does it line up with the Word of God?) Gospel music has ministered to me on numerous occasions, sometimes by communicating the answers that I need, and other times by simply shifting my focus from self-pity to praise. It is impossible to focus on both God and His goodness and your problems at the same time. The key is to stay focused on His Word. Whether you choose Gospel music, Christian teaching tapes, or meditating on Scripture, the key is to keep your mind on Him (Psalm 26:3).

Additionally, don't overlook the power of church attendance in developing your faith and restoring your soul. Often, when we are going through difficult times in life, our first inclination is to stop going to church (if we've been attending regularly) or to wait until we "get it together" to begin attending. Both are tricks of the enemy to keep us away from the power of the preached Word, corporate prayer, praise, and worship. I have learned to push even harder during those times when my flesh shouts, "I'm too tired," "I'm depressed," "I'm sick of church folk," "I don't have to go to church...God knows my heart," "I'll go next week," or some other self-defeating confession.

I have learned to push my way through these excuses. It is important that I stay connected to the church, God's people, and His Word. I know too well that I cannot afford to wait until I get it together to go to church. Rather, I need to go for the strength, wisdom, and inspiration to get it together, and you do, too!

WITH THE SUPPORT OF
FRIENDS AND FAMILY

I thank God daily for loving, praying, and supportive friends and family. It is nice to know that someone "has my back" at all times, and it is always easier to get my groove back in the company of those who genuinely care about me. The Bible says,

Two people can accomplish more than twice as
much as one; they get a better return for their labor.
If one person falls, the other can reach out and help.
But people who are alone when they fall are in real trouble...
A person standing alone can be defeated,
but two can stand back-to-back and conquer....

ECCLESIASTES 4:9-10 AND 12

God designed us to need fellowship. We were not created to live in isolation. We serve God and others through relationships. The enemy is aware of the need for godly associations and their benefits to us. Consequently, he seeks to place conflict, strife, jealousy, and envy in our relationships. We must recognize his tricks and work diligently to nurture and maintain our godly associations.

I feel sorry for the women I meet who proudly proclaim that they have no girlfriends because they don't trust women. My heart goes out to them because I understand (from experience) the pain of betrayal, the disappointment of backbiting, and the sting of jealousy. My heart also hurts for them because I know the sanctuary found in sisterhood, the protection found in prayer partners, and the comfort found in camaraderie. I thank God that the decoys sent by the devil did not cause me to give up on true, God-ordained friendships and relationships. We all need friends who will be there for us during the good times and the bad.

I am not naive enough to think that everyone that I meet can become a "friend." As a matter of fact, I am very prayerful and careful about who I allow into the intimate places in my life. I also encourage you to be selective (Proverbs 12:26). If you will allow Him, God will surround you with people who have your best interests at heart. I believe that our friendships are purposed. God does not place people in our lives for us to merely hang out with them and have a good time. Although good times are a fringe benefit of friendship, the purpose is always larger. We must lift all of our friendships up to God in prayer, seeking the larger purpose.

At the beginning of the Book of Ruth, the women's relationship appears to be a simple in-law association, but God had a much greater plan for this divine connection. God used Naomi's wisdom and selflessness in friendship to steer Ruth toward the awesome purpose and plan that He had for Ruth's life. Ruth's loyalty to and love for her mother-in-law was not just a blessing to Naomi; God richly blessed Ruth in return. Neither of the women would have guessed that their friendship was tied to their destinies.

BE CAREFUL IF YOU HAVE SURROUNDED YOURSELF WITH PEOPLE WHO ALWAYS TELL YOU WHAT IS PLEASING TO YOUR EARS.

True friendships are mutually rewarding. The rewards are not always packaged the way we would like to receive them, but they are nevertheless beneficial. True friends add value to our lives. They are not "yes people." They don't tell you what they think you want to hear; instead, they tell you what they believe you need to hear. Be careful if you have surrounded yourself with people who always tell you what is pleasing to your ears. You may be positioned for a hard fall.

I thank God for the friends that He has placed in my life. We often joke about our "willingness" to tell each other the truth. We do not gloat in pointing out each other's shortcomings; rather, we love, respect, and trust one another enough to be open and honest in all areas. Though the truth usually stings momentarily and sometimes even hurts, I am always better off as a result of their loving reprimands and constructive confrontations (Proverbs 28:23).

As a woman of God, it is important to surround yourself with friends who are also committed to Him. Friends who will stretch you to become the best that you can be. Friends who, if necessary, will tell you the whole truth. Friends who are slow to share their opinions, but quick to share what "thus says the Lord." Friends whose advice is seldom, "Girl, if I were you…" and often, "Girl, the Bible says…"

I don't know about you, but I need friends who are going to pray for me and remind me of God's Word in challenging situations. Friends who will provide a shoulder to cry on, a listening ear, and godly counsel when needed.

FOCUSED ON THE FUTURE

My very first car accident taught me a lesson about driving and about life... *You cannot successfully move forward while continuously looking backward.*

I vividly remember the day I wrecked my mom's powder blue Cutlass Supreme. I begged her to allow me to drive the car to my job at a neighborhood department store, with the promise that I would be very careful. Unfortunately, I was still in that stage of life (those teenage years) when impressing others was very important to me. While cruising through the parking lot, I noticed a group of friends staring as I drove by, so I turned to smile and wave. I never saw the other vehicle coming.

86

This is exactly what happens sometimes in our lives. We spend so much time looking back, focusing on past hurts, disappointments, setbacks, and even past accomplishments that we never see the "crash" coming until the damage has been done. Countless marriages end in ruins because one or both parties remain focused on "the way it used to be." Many women suffer from low self-esteem and depression, unable to love and value themselves because they are stuck, longing for the size six figures they once had. Many of us never experience the peace, purpose, and abundance that God promises because we remain stuck in the "if I coulda, I woulda, I shoulda" stages of life.

When the Book of Ruth opens, the two desperate and destitute widows are embarking upon a journey to another country looking for restoration and hope. Neither of them knew exactly what the future held, but both were willing to release the bitter realities of the days gone by in exchange for new beginnings. Both women took a huge risk, walking away from the familiar to step into the unknown. Though Bethlehem was not new to Naomi, it held new possibilities. We hear her hopelessness in verses 20-21, but in the very next verse, we begin to see a shift in her situation.

"Don't call me Naomi," she told them. "Instead, call me Mara, for the Almighty has made life very bitter for me. I went away full, but the LORD has brought me home empty. Why should you call me Naomi when the LORD has caused me to suffer and the Almighty has sent such tragedy?"

So Naomi returned, and Ruth the Moabitess,
her daughter-in-law, with her, who returned from the
country of Moab. And they came to Bethlehem at the
beginning of barley harvest.

RUTH 1:20-22

We do not have to know a great deal about harvest seasons to conclude that harvest time is a time of reaping and increase. Almost instantly, we begin to see Ruth and Naomi's season change!

What changes have you been waiting for, hoping for, and praying for? Are you focused on the changes, or is your focus stuck on your present state of being or even your past? Allow me to share a personal example. My husband Larry and I have a loving, trusting, and Christ-centered relationship. Has it always been that way? No. It started off well, but a few months into our engagement, it seemed that all hell broke loose. Like my first car accident, I never saw it coming; what a blow! Let me summarize the story by telling you that my heart was broken into what felt like a million pieces. The private pain was piercing, and to add insult to injury, I had to deal with the public pain of announcing my broken engagement. I was over forty, had never been married, and had a truckload of girlfriends who shared this mid-life, single status. My engagement was the ray of hope for which they had all been waiting. Furthermore, "somehow" the exciting news of it seemed to have traveled faster than the Gospel, reaching the uttermost parts of the earth! Everybody knew that I was engaged to be married, and I had to be the one to break the news that the wedding was off.

From the day Larry and I met, I prayed fervently for God to reveal His purpose and plan for the relationship. I felt certain that I had met the man of my dreams. However, one "wrong turn" sent our relationship down what could have been a road of no return. I called the wedding off and ended the relationship. This immediate reaction reflected the "zero tolerance law" that I applied to relationships. This unyielding, unforgiving, and unhealthy mindset was a result of my past. Unfortunately, I had seen and experienced more than enough bad relationships. Clearly, we should learn from experiences, or we will continue to make the same mistakes. However, life's lessons should increase our wisdom, not our *baggage*.

I thank God for my husband's perseverance and prayers during our engagement period. I am eternally grateful that God did not allow our relationship to be destroyed while we went through the process of healing, restoration, and change. Instead, what the enemy meant for evil, God used for our good. We both learned valuable lessons that have helped to develop us as individuals and strengthen us as a couple. Both of us had to face some real and challenging issues in our lives. Of course, I was well aware of all of *his issues*, but the revelation of some of *mine* was shocking!

In order for our relationship to grow and develop into the wonderful marriage that it is today, we had to set our minds on the future that God had promised us. Both of us had sought His guidance, heard His voice, and knew that our destinies were tied together. We, or shall I say I, had to decide to throw off the weight of disappointments and unforgiveness.

I had to decide to release the past and direct my thoughts toward the future. This was not easy. Change, consistency, and commitment were required. First, I prayed and asked God to help me. I knew our relationship was ordained by Him, and I knew that He would help me if I asked. Secondly, *I started thinking about what I was always thinking about.* (This is one of my favorite lessons from author and speaker Joyce Meyer.) If I found my thoughts focused on negative events and details from the past, I immediately replaced them with faith-filled thoughts of our future.

My story, like that of Ruth's and Naomi's, is an amazing illustration of Isaiah 61. One tearful night during our broken engagement, I awakened to find this chapter lying open in the Bible on my bed. I held fast to its message of restoration and began to confess its promises. And true to His Word, God gave me joy for my mourning, prosperity for my shame, and double for my trouble! He gave me my *groove* back – the right way. I had to make up my mind to forget about the past and press on toward the future. I am so glad that I did!

THOUGHT QUESTIONS

1. Are you in your *groove* – a place of joy, peace, and contentment? If so, which factors play essential roles in your state of being?

_____

_____

_____

_____

_____

_____

_____

If not, what seems to be missing?

_____

_____

_____

_____

_____

2. Do you have godly friends or family members with whom you can share your joys, sorrows, hurts, and disappointments? If so, can these people be counted on to tell you the truth, not just what you want to hear? Describe a situation in which you have benefited from "the truth."

_____

_____

_____

_____

_____

_____

_____

_____

_____

If not, what's preventing you from developing godly relationships? Pray and ask God to bring godly people into your life.

_____

_____

_____

_____

_____

3. Which past hurts, disappointments, or setbacks are you having difficulty releasing? How is holding on to the past keeping you from moving forward?

_____

_____

_____

_____

_____

_____

_____

_____

_____

4. Is there anyone in your present or past that you need to forgive? What's keeping you from forgiving him or her? Decide today to release yourself from this paralyzing hold through forgiveness. Ask God to help you.

_____

_____

_____

_____

_____

5. What did God reveal to you through this chapter?

_____

_____

_____

_____

_____

_____

_____

_____

What will you do with these revelations? Which changes will you make? Which actions will you take?

_____

_____

_____

_____

_____

_____

_____

_____

CONFESSIONS

Though I experience difficulties and at times grow weary,
I will never give up. My spirit is renewed daily.
I'm not dismayed by my present troubles because I know that
they won't last very long. They will actually benefit me in the
long run. So I don't focus on what I see right now; rather, I
look forward to the unseen. My troubles will soon pass,
and the joys to come will last forever.
(2 Corinthians 4:16-18)

I rejoice in the Lord at all times. I don't worry about anything
or allow stress or depression to control me; instead, I take
all of my concerns to God in prayer, with thanksgiving in my
heart for all that He has done and all that He will do for me.
God in turn gives me His indescribable peace.
This peace guards my heart and my mind.
(Philippians 4:6-7)

I choose to let go of my past. I will not dwell on the mistakes,
the hurts, or even the accomplishments of yesterday.
God is doing a brand-new thing in my life.
I'm not there yet, but I can see it by faith. He's making a way
for me where there seems to be no way. I press forward
toward all that He has in store for me.
(Isaiah 43:18-19, Philippians 3:13-14)

I surround myself with godly friends
who give me good advice.
(Proverbs 12:26)

I do not give place to bitterness, rage, harsh words,
slander, or other malicious behavior.
Instead, I am kind, tenderhearted, and forgiving.
(Ephesians 4:31)

God has blessed me with a double portion for my inheritance.
I have received double honor and prosperity for all of my
troubles and shame. He has turned my mourning into
dancing and covered me with everlasting joy.
(Isaiah 61:7 and Psalm 30:10)

Which point from this chapter speaks directly to one of your personal situations? Search God's Word for relevant promises and write a faith confession concerning the matter.

_____

_____

_____

_____

_____

_____

_____

_____

_____

_____

_____

_____

_____

_____

_____

CHAPTER SIX

LOOK FROM WHERE YOU ARE

"What could be worse than being born without sight?
Being born with sight and no vision."

— HELEN KELLER —

*S*omeone struggling with despair once asked me, "What do I have to look forward to?" I don't remember my response, but hopefully, my answer was led by the Holy Spirit. Today, my unequivocal answer to this question is, "You can look forward to whatever you look forward to!"

What do I mean by this? I believe John Richardson explains it best:

> *"When it comes to the future, there are three kinds of people: those who let it happen, those who make it happen, and those who sit back and wonder what happened."*

Life happens, but we play a significant role in determining the details of what happens along the way. What we believe and conceive largely determines what we achieve in life. Those who *make things happen* take the time to think about the future. As my pastor Joel Osteen so powerfully teaches, they develop "visions of victory" for their lives. In other words, your future will look a lot like you envision it.

Vision is defined as a mental picture of a preferable future. It is a mental image of what is to be achieved. Throughout the ages, many experts and scholars have taught on and written about vision. Therefore, I will not attempt to redo that which has been done so well, but I will share a few life-changing lessons that I have discovered regarding God's vision for our lives.

Proverbs 29:18 tells us that without vision, people perish. When applied to daily living, this passage speaks volumes. Without vision, life becomes meaningless, empty, and nonproductive.

Vision adds purpose, focus, and excitement to life. It gives you the strength to tie a knot and hold on when the present circumstances would otherwise tempt you to let go. Vision allows you to create a mental picture of an existence different from your present state of being. Unfortunately, many people stumble through life without vision.

VISION ADDS PURPOSE, FOCUS, AND EXCITEMENT TO LIFE.

They allow their narrow focus on surviving the moment to limit their desire for and access to the abundant life that God promises. People without vision go through the motions of life without dreams and expectations. They become stagnant and complacent, accepting whatever comes their way. Without vision, it is difficult, if not impossible, to move strategically and successfully to a desired place in life.

God has an awesome vision for each of our lives. His vision for our future is filled with hope, purpose, and possibilities.

"For I know the plans I have for you," says the Lord.
"They are plans for good and not for disaster,
to give you a future and a hope."

JEREMIAH 29:11

99

Years ago, after fully discovering the power of this passage in Jeremiah, I made up my mind that I was created to thrive, not to merely survive. I knew that there was more to life than I was experiencing at that time, and I wanted it. I sought God's guidance and prayed that He would give me a new lease on life. What He gave me was His vision for my life. He began to unfold, and still continues to unfold, His purpose and plans for me. Immediately, I began to see myself experiencing and accomplishing things that I had never imagined.

I believe two of the reasons God gives us vision are to encourage us and to keep us focused. We can see this illustrated in the story of Abraham (Genesis 11-25). In chapter 13, we meet Abraham at a place in his journey where he needed a vision from God for his life. He had obeyed God, left his comfort zone, and stepped out into unknown territory. He had also, reluctantly but necessarily, parted ways with his nephew Lot, whom he loved dearly. Abraham's mental picture of his future was probably blurry and uncertain, but God had an awesome plan for him.

The Lord said to Abram after Lot had left him,

Lift up now your eyes and look from the place where you are,

northward and southward and eastward and westward;

For all the land which you see I will give to you

and to your posterity forever.

And I will make your descendants like the dust of the earth,

so that if a man could count the dust of the earth,

then could your descendants also be counted.

Arise, walk through the land, the length of it and the

breadth of it, for I will give it to you.

GENESIS 13:14-17 (AMP)

Likewise, God has a plan for you and me, and He wants to reveal it to us. I've learned by studying the life of Abraham that if we are ultimately going to live out God's perfect plan for our lives, we must be able to see what He sees. We must lift up our eyes, look around, and look beyond where we are. Unfortunately, the enemy uses the circumstances of life to distort our vision, but I have discovered a process by which God's vision for my life is transmitted clearly and effectively. Whenever I'm seeking God's will or vision for me in a particular situation, I put on my trifocals. These are not natural lenses but rather spiritual eyewear designed to give me supernatural vision and faith-based focus. My trifocals allow me to look up, around, and beyond and to see clearly in all three directions. Now, put on your spiritual eyewear and...

LOOK UP

Rick Warren, in his very popular book *The Purpose - Driven Life*, wrote...

> *The search for purpose of life has puzzled people for thousands of years. That's because we typically begin at the wrong starting point — ourselves. We ask self-centered questions like "What do I want to be? What should I do with my life? What are my goals, my ambitions, my dreams for my future?" But focusing on ourselves will never reveal our life's purpose. The Bible says, "It's God who directs the lives of His creatures; everyone's life is in His power."*
> *...you cannot arrive at your life's purpose by starting with a focus on yourself. You must begin with God, your Creator. You exist only because God wills that you exist. You were made by God and for God — and until you understand that, life will never make sense. It is only in God that we discover our origin, our identity, our meaning, our purpose,*

*our significance, and our destiny. Every other path leads
to a dead-end.[1]*

Unfortunately, many of us never receive God's vision for
our lives because we never pursue it. We waste time and energy
painting our own pictures of "success" and then become frustrated
and discouraged when all of the pieces never
seem to come together. I have lost track of how
many businesses, relationships, and other ideas I
have conjured up in my own mind only to later
realize – after much toil and many tears – that
God never intended them for me. Most of them
were good ideas, but they were not God's ideas
for me.

> EVERY GOOD
> THING IS NOT
> NECESSARILY
> A GOD THING
> – FOR YOU.

Please stop and take notes here. Every good thing is not
necessarily a God thing – for you. I struggled with this notion for
some time before coming to terms with it. All good and perfect gifts
come from God (James 1:17). So why did I find myself struggling
with good things? God's answer to me was simple: "Just because
it's good does not mean that it's good for you." Let me give you
some examples:

- Have you ever been introduced to a gentleman who
  was known by all to be a *good* man, but you knew in
  your spirit that he was not your man?
- What about those *good* deals? Have you ever purchased
  something that was on sale, knowing that even the
  incredible sale price was outside of your budget?
- How many times have you been disappointed when
  you didn't get that *good* job, only to later learn that the
  position had been downsized or something similarly
  shocking?

Throughout the Bible, we see God moving in extraordinary ways in the lives of those men and women who sought His presence and guidance. We can save ourselves countless hours and much heartache by looking up and seeking His plan for our lives. He wants to guide, protect, and bless us.

But this is what I commanded them, saying,
"Obey My voice, and I will be your God, and you shall be My people.
And walk in all the ways that I have commanded you,
that it may be well with you."

JEREMIAH 7:23 (NKJV)

We can seek God's vision for our lives through prayer, meditation, worship, and praise. This requires setting aside quality time to get into His presence. I suggest that you schedule a daily appointment with God. You must block out the distractions and guard this time with Him as you would any of your other "important" appointments.

I'm reminded of the powerful testimony of a young woman named Diane. Seeking God's purpose and plan for her life, she attended a church conference workshop in Houston entitled "Is God in Your Palm Pilot?" Convicted and impacted by the workshop, she returned to her home in New York with a renewed commitment to her daily devotion and meditation time. One morning while reading the Bible, she felt God's presence and guidance like never before. The soft, assuring voice of God led her to read and meditate on the following passage:

When you pass through the waters, I will be with you;
and through the rivers, they shall not overflow you.
When you walk through the fire, you shall not be
burned, nor shall the flame scorch you.

ISAIAH 43:2 (NKJV)

Diane became so engrossed in meditation that she lost track of time and ran late for work. Hurrying to the Twin Towers where her son attended daycare, she had no idea of what she was about to encounter. Upon reaching the Twin Towers, she discovered to her paralyzing shock that both buildings had just been struck by two highjacked jets. Yes, it was the morning of September 11, 2001! I sat in complete awe as she told this very moving story.

Diane's time with God on the morning of September 11 literally saved her and her son from danger. God wants to reveal secret things to us. He wants to warn us of impending dangers. He wants to direct us in our daily affairs.

> "Call to Me, and I will answer you,
> and show you great and mighty things,
> which you do not know."
>
> JEREMIAH 33:3

I am convinced that the time we spend with God is essential to our receiving revelations of His purposes and plans for our lives. Unfortunately, through self-sufficiency, busyness, and other destructive tactics, the enemy continuously seeks to create division in our relationship with God. However, we must not succumb to the enemy's schemes. Our responsibilities are to look up, to spend time with God, and to develop an intimate and personal relationship with Him so that we are able to clearly hear and recognize His voice.

> I will stand upon my watch...and will watch to
> see what he will say unto me...
>
> HABAKKUK 2:1 (KJV)

LOOK AROUND

In Genesis 13:14-17, God instructed Abraham to look northward, southward, eastward, and westward. An essential step in reaching your preferred future is to look around, to get a clear picture and understanding of where you are right now.

I have a close friend who is severely "directionally challenged." It is hard for me to fathom how she is able to travel around her neighborhood, not to mention the city, without a very high-tech and user-friendly navigation system. On numerous occasions, I have received frantic calls from her seeking directions to rescue her from some "lost position." Usually, one of my first questions is, "Where are you?" Her frequent response is, "I don't know!" In these situations, I could not begin to help my friend reach her destination until she could first tell me her location.

In order for us to experience the realization of our visions and dreams, we must first discover our location. We must look around and examine our surroundings before beginning to map out a plan for moving from where we are to where we want to be. If we fail to do this, we expend vast amounts of time and energy wandering in circles.

Let's look at this concept practically. I've often heard friends at the beginning of a new diet or exercise program say that they have no idea how much they weigh. Neither are they aware of their body measurements. I find this astonishing. I will assume this approach works for them, but it would never work for me. Although I believe daily weigh-ins and constant focus on the weight can be counterproductive, I also believe that a clear assessment of the situation is important. An up-front evaluation gives you the barometer by which to measure your progress.

I recently implemented a plan to eliminate all of my credit card debt. My first step in this process was to *look around*. I needed a clear picture of my financial condition. It would not have been enough to simply guess my credit card balances. I needed exact figures. I had to courageously take the time to carefully assess the situation. I say "courageously" because it was painful to *really* look at my situation. (The truth can "hurt" at first, but it will set you free.) I had to assess the situation in order to determine the real problem. I had to look at my spending habits and face the reality that my expenditures were exceeding my income. Then, I had to develop a plan for the successful management of my finances. I could have taken the haphazard approach that I had taken many times in the past, but this time, I was serious. No more cutting up the credit cards, only to walk up to the customer service counter for a replacement. No more impulsive purchasing.

WHO OR WHAT AROUND YOU IS PREVENTING YOU FROM MOVING TO THE NEXT PLACE?

I hope you're beginning to understand the importance of *looking around*. Before I move on, I must mention one other very important area that demands attention. Who or what around you is preventing you from moving to the next place?

I find it interesting that Abraham received a clear vision from the Lord *after* Lot left him (Genesis 13:14-17). Sometimes we have to part ways with people and circumstances that keep us from reaching our full potential. I call them "bubble busters."

I can remember loving bubble-gum as a child. Not only did I love the taste, but I also loved blowing bubbles. I would sit and practice blowing the biggest, most beautiful bubbles. One of my friends would marvel at my masterpieces and even assist me by attempting to shield my bubbles from the wind or anything that would cause them to burst. Another friend who could not blow bubbles got a thrill out of sneaking up behind me and smashing my big, beautiful bubbles right in my face. If this sounds like a ridiculous example, I ask you to seriously consider it. How many times have you been excited about a vision or goal, only to share it with someone who smashes it in your face with their negative words or blatant lack of support?

A few years ago, the Lord gave me the vision for an innovative, Christian television talk show. I shared this vision with friends and associates in an attempt to gain the professional and financial support that I needed to produce a demo tape. Overall, the support that I received was overwhelming. Family members, friends, and colleagues shared the time, talent, and resources needed to produce the tape. I was humbled and tremendously blessed by their unselfish commitment to "my" vision.

God used this project to show me the fundamental value of true friendships. Through it, He also allowed me to recognize several unhealthy alliances. The most heartbreaking revelation involved a person I considered a friend. After another very close friend suggested that I host a vision casting party to solicit financial support for the project, I shared the idea with Ann (the name has been changed to protect the guilty) for feedback. Ann emphatically stated that she would never attend such a function... and would surely never give her money to support someone else's vision. *Pop! Right in the face.*

To add insult to injury, another "friend" took on the mission (for which he was not professionally qualified) of advising me of all that I lacked to make it in "the business." His message was basically "don't even try it because you're not going to make it." *Pop! Right in the face!*

Both of these "bubble busters" were temporarily deflating, but thank God, neither had permanent effects. Like the little girl who had learned to meticulously pull the gum from her face, put it back in her mouth, and continue to blow bubbles, I kept going. God took what the enemy meant for evil in this situation and used it for my good. Instead of allowing these "bubble busters" to slow me down or stop me, they actually added fuel to my fire. I was determined to prove them wrong.

> WE CANNOT REALISTICALLY EXPECT EVERYONE TO SEE AND SUPPORT OUR VISIONS.

When you look around, are the people in your inner circle *builders* or *busters?* Are they genuinely excited about and supportive of your bubbles (visions, goals, and dreams)? Do they encourage you to blow bigger bubbles and then do what it takes to support you in your endeavors? Or are they busters who enjoy seeing your bubbles burst in your face or, worse yet, pop your bubbles with their negative energy, actions, and comments?

We cannot realistically expect everyone to see and support our visions. Unfortunately, some will take more pleasure in sabotaging than celebrating our success. You owe it to yourself to take a good look at those around you – family members, colleagues, friends, significant others, and business partners. Do you trust those closest to you? Do you feel that they have your best interests at heart? We have to know when to cut the ties. Often, we see the dysfunction, but we hang on, hoping desperately for a change in them. We sometimes fail to see that the change needed must be in us.

The time that you spend looking around will prove to be very productive. Spend some time each day in reflection. Take a few minutes to simply assess your day. Ask yourself some key questions.

- *Where am I?*
- *Am I moving in the right direction?*
- *Which roadblocks are along my path?*

- *Which detours must I take to get around these roadblocks?*
- *Who is with me?*
- *Are those who are with me builders or busters?*
- *Am I a builder or a buster in the lives of those around me?*

Regarding the last question above, it is also important to note, one of the most productive things that you can do while waiting for your own dreams and visions to manifest is to help someone else realize his or hers. In other words, the investment of your time, talent, resources, and prayers in the fulfillment of someone else's dream will reap great returns in the manifestation of your own.

The Bible is clear on its message of sowing and reaping. We reap what we sow (2 Corinthians 9:6). Furthermore, it is a natural law. If you want a harvest, you must plant seeds.

If you give, you will receive.
Your gift will return to you in full measure, pressed down,
shaken together to make room for more, and running over.
Whatever measure you use in giving
– large or small – it will be used to measure
what is given back to you.

LUKE 6:38

When God first gave me the vision to start my own consulting business, I did not know where to begin. I had neither the knowledge nor the resources to begin such a venture. The one thing I did have was *good seed in the ground.* Over the years, I had invested much of my time, energy, and resources into helping others build businesses and non-profit organizations, promote products and services, and reach personal goals. My motive for these investments was never the return, but God is faithful to His Word.

Nothing about my decision to launch a new business made sense at this time in my life. I did not have an office, equipment, furnishings, or money. All I had was peace in my heart regarding the venture and a promise from God, which proved to be sufficient. I had always heard the saying "Where God guides, He provides," so I stepped out on faith, believing that He would provide everything that I needed to be successful in business.

Many people stepped forward, most of them unsolicited, to assist me with this God-inspired venture. I was blessed with a wealth of inspiration, information, resources, and referrals. Every time the enemy attempted to discourage me or remind me of what I did not have, the Lord would send a "builder" to encourage me and to remind me that He was in control.

I will never forget going shopping with a friend who was purchasing a computer for her new home. This friend was tremendously blessed financially and had recently retired at the age of 35. As we strolled through the computer store surveying equipment, I thought to myself, "Why am I looking? I need a computer, but I can't afford anything in here." But I did not allow my lack of finances to extinguish the excitement that I felt. After my friend and I selected computers, printers, and accessories, we realized that her vehicle was too small to transport any of the boxes. Due to my lack of finances, I was relieved when the store clerk suggested that we place the merchandise on hold. I prayed that I would somehow receive the money to purchase the items before the deadline. The next day, my friend called and asked me to return to the store with her to help pick up her equipment. My initial thought was, "I don't want to do that. I can't purchase *my* computer today. Why should I go?" But I did not allow this negative feeling to override the positive desire to simply help a friend.

As my friend stood at the counter completing the transaction, the clerk called me up and asked me to select an e-mail address. I responded, "No, I would like to leave my items on hold for a while longer." He replied, "Your friend just purchased a computer for you." In fact, not only had she purchased a computer, but she had also purchased a printer. Both were upgraded editions of the models I had placed on hold! This was an act of kindness I will never forget and a testament to the benefit of sowing and reaping.

Similarly, another friend helped me to secure my first major contract. She *just happened* to be in the position to provide a personal recommendation of my character and competence. I emphasized *just happened* because I am reminded of a powerful sermon preached by Bishop T.D. Jakes entitled, "Nothing Just Happens." I believe that God purposed and positioned my friend to be at that place, at that time. Like Esther and others in the Bible, many of us are purposefully placed in positions where God can use us to bless others. This friend has since been promoted to a higher and more financially rewarding position within her company. She often tells of how there were many candidates for her new position who were more qualified. She is undoubtedly reaping what she has sown.

> WHILE YOU ARE WAITING FOR YOUR BLESSING, BE A BLESSING TO SOMEONE ELSE.

I have been on both sides of the sowing and reaping equation and could share countless testimonies that illustrate the legitimacy of this principle. Trust me when I tell you that what you do for others, God will do for you. While you are waiting for your blessing, be a blessing to someone else. Volunteer your time and computer skills to help someone who is starting a new business. Assist an aspiring author by proofreading his or her manuscript. Baby-sit for a friend who needs to work longer hours to complete a project. Offer to run errands, paint the office, file, or simply distribute business cards for someone who is beginning a new venture. Be a *builder*, not a *buster*.

LOOK BEYOND

Jesus came so that we could have life and have it more abundantly (John 10:10). What does this passage really mean? Many of us cannot begin to envision the abundant life God desires for us because we cannot see beyond our present circumstances. We cannot see the abundance in our future because our focus is on the lack, the obstacles, the pain, and the shortcomings of today. In order for us to reach the place of peace, purpose, and abundance in our lives, we must be able to look beyond our fears, our limitations, our insecurities, and our pasts. We must have vision.

IN ORDER FOR US TO REACH THE PLACE OF PEACE, PURPOSE, AND ABUNDANCE IN OUR LIVES, WE MUST BE ABLE TO LOOK BEYOND OUR FEARS, OUR LIMITATIONS, OUR INSECURITIES, AND OUR PASTS.

In Genesis 13:14, God instructed Abraham to look beyond the place where he stood. He needed Abraham to have a mental picture of the future promised to him. Like Abraham, we have received numerous promises from God. He has literally given us His Word regarding our health, our finances, our relationships, our future, and other matters that concern us. Unlike Abraham, many of us do not respond to God with obedience and trust. We allow our current situations to cloud our minds with doubt and unbelief. This cloudiness is detrimental to living life with vision and purpose.

Looking *beyond* requires steps of faith. Remember the definition of faith found in Hebrews 11:1. The New King James Version states, "Now faith is the substance of things hoped for, the evidence of things not seen." The New Living Translation provides an even clearer definition: "What is faith? It is the confident assurance that what we hope for is going to happen. It is the evidence of things we cannot yet see."

112

Abraham possessed this kind of faith. He was able to step out of his comfort zone without knowing exactly where he was going. He and Sarah were able to look beyond her barrenness and believe God for the child that He promised.

> It was by faith that Abraham obeyed when
> God called him to leave home and go to another land
> that God would give him as his inheritance.
> He went without knowing where he was going. And even
> when he reached the land God promised him, he lived
> there by faith – for he was like a foreigner, living in a tent.
> And so did Isaac and Jacob, to whom God gave the same
> promise. Abraham did this because he was confidently
> looking forward to a city with eternal foundations,
> a city designed and built by God.
>
> It was by faith that Sarah together with Abraham
> was able to have a child, even though they were too old
> and Sarah was barren. Abraham believed that
> God would keep his promise.
> And so a whole nation came from this one man...
> HEBREWS 11:8-12

Like Abraham, we must not allow our present situations to delay or distract us. How many times have you felt the Lord leading you into new territory, showing you a brighter future, but your vision was blurred by doubt and unbelief? Do any of the following confessions sound familiar?

I can't see myself making that kind of money.

I don't see how I'll ever get out of this mess.

I just can't see this marriage getting any better.

I don't see them promoting me into that position.

I can't see them hiring me with no experience.

I just can't see it!

You can counter these confessions with one of my favorite Bible passages:

> God is not a man, that he should lie.
> He is not a human, that he should change his mind.
> Has he ever spoken and failed to act?
> Has he ever promised and not carried it through?
>
> NUMBERS 23:19

I confess this passage frequently, reminding myself that God is not a liar, and His Word is not fiction. He is faithful, and He is true to His Word. If He said it, I can believe it.

Too often, we sabotage our success with our negative thoughts and confessions. If we hope to see the dreams and visions God has given us fulfilled in our lives, we must see them by faith and believe God to bring them to pass. I have developed two simple habits that help me to guard the dreams and visions that God gives me until they are manifested in my life.

Habit 1: Meditating on God's Word

The Bible is full of God's promises regarding every area of our lives. We are instructed to read and obey His Word in order to be successful.

> This Book of the Law shall not depart out of
> your mouth, but you shall meditate on it day and
> night, that you may observe
> and do according to all that is written in it.
> For then you shall make your way prosperous,
> and then you shall deal wisely and have good success.
>
> JOSHUA 1:8 (AMP)

I have developed the habit of searching God's Word for promises and instructions relative to my dreams and visions. I record these promises and instructions, reviewing, confessing, and meditating on them regularly. I suggest that you do the same. Surround yourself with the Word. Record scriptures in a journal, on poster boards, on note cards, or anywhere you can view them on a daily basis. Guard your dreams and visions by filling your mind and your conversations with the Word of God, leaving no room for negative, self-defeating thoughts.

Habit 2: Writing the Vision

The Bible instructs us to "write the vision" (Habakkuk 2:2). I do this by creating pictures of the visions and dreams that God places in my spirit. I have constructed what I call a "Vision Book." This is a photo album/scrapbook that I use to store pictures, scriptures, confessions, and notes that pertain to my visions and dreams. I have found that regular review of the contents of my Vision Book helps to keep my visions and dreams alive. These "faith pictures" help me to look beyond my present circumstances and envision myself in the depicted situations.

My home was furnished in my Vision Book long before I actually saved the down payment for it. My wedding was planned in my Vision Book long before I was introduced to my husband. In both of these cases and in many others, I have been amazed at how similar the actual manifestations of the visions and dreams have been to the faith pictures that I created.

I encourage you to create your own Vision Book. Imagine what the fulfillment of your visions and dreams will look like, and depict them in your book. Include a picture of the office building or property where you would like to set up your new business, pictures of places you dream of visiting, a copy of your monthly budget (completed by using your *desired* income), and scriptures of God's promises pertaining to your vision.

If you think the idea of creating a Vision Book is a little absurd, read Habakkuk 2:2-3. God instructed Habakkuk to write the vision plainly and to wait patiently for its fulfillment. The Message Bible provides a vivid translation:

And then God answered:
"Write this. Write what you see. Write it out in big block
letters so that it can be read on the run. This vision-message
is a witness pointing to what's coming.
It aches for the coming – it can hardly wait!
And it doesn't lie.
If it seems slow in coming, wait. It's on the way.
It will come right on time."

The realization of your visions and dreams are probably closer than you think. Keep them alive!

THOUGHT QUESTIONS

1. What seemingly *good things* have you prayed for, only to later realize that they weren't *God things – for you*?

_____

_____

_____

_____

_____

_____

_____

_____

_____

_____

_____

_____

_____

_____

_____

2. Is spending time with God a priority in your daily schedule? If so, describe your quiet time with him. (Do you look forward to it? What do you do? Where? When? For how long?) If not, pray and ask God to help you develop this daily discipline.

_____

_____

_____

_____

_____

_____

_____

_____

_____

3. Who are the "builders" in your life? How do they encourage or support you?

_____

_____

_____

_____

_____

_____

_____

_____

_____

_____

_____

_____

_____

_____

4. Who are the "busters" in your life? How are they hindering
    your progress toward your goals?

_____

_____

_____

_____

_____

_____

_____

_____

_____

_____

_____

_____

_____

5. Where are you along the path to realizing a major dream or vision that God has given you? Are you moving forward, or are you stalled? If you're stalled, what is your plan of action for getting back on the right track?

_____

_____

_____

_____

_____

_____

_____

6. What did God reveal to you through this chapter?

_____

_____

_____

_____

_____

_____

_____

What will you do with these revelations? Which changes will you make? Which actions will you take?

_____

_____

_____

_____

_____

_____

_____

_____

CONFESSIONS

My greatest desire is to dwell in the
presence of the Lord every day of my life.
(Psalm 27:4)

The Holy Spirit helps me to fulfill my God-given dreams and
visions. He gives me the wisdom, the guidance, and the
power to achieve my goals. He knows God's will for my life,
and He prays for me in harmony with that will.
(John 16:7, 13-15 and Romans 8:27)

God has good thoughts about me. His plans for me include
hope and a prosperous future. The Lord makes Himself
available to me. He listens carefully to my prayers and
answers them. (Jeremiah 29:11)

Even when the facts look discouraging, I still trust God.
I do not dwell on my circumstances; rather, I look beyond my
limitations, staying focused on His power.
I believe God's Word, and I have faith in His ability to do
exactly what He promised.
(Romans 4:19-21)

God blesses me abundantly, and I am a blessing to others.
I cheerfully give of my time, gifts, talents, and resources,
and God faithfully pours new blessings and abundant
resources into my life.
(Genesis 12:2 and Luke 6:38)

God has given me an awesome vision. Though it seems
slow in coming, I will wait patiently for it. It will not be late;
rather, it will be fulfilled at His appointed time. I am confident
of this because God is faithful.
(Habakkuk 2:3 and Numbers 23:19)

Which point from this chapter speaks directly to one of your personal situations? Search God's Word for relevant promises and write a faith confession concerning the matter.

_____

_____

_____

_____

_____

_____

_____

_____

_____

_____

_____

_____

_____

_____

_____

_____

_____

_____

_____

_____

CHAPTER SEVEN

DRAW THE LINE

You will never change
that which you tolerate.

– MIKE MURDOCK –

$\mathcal{S}$ome of my most vivid childhood memories include the period when my family resided in what was then called "the projects." Depending on your age, you may or may not be familiar with this term. The new, politically correct term used to define these dwellings is "affordable housing developments." Although the name has changed, the essence remains the same.

In the projects, it was not uncommon to find yourself in some kind of battle. One thing I remember is that somebody always drew a line in the dirt. The line represented territory or boundary. One could shout a host of threats from his or her side of the line, but once the line was crossed, as today's kids say, "It was on!"

The familiar Bible story of David and Goliath is told in 1 Samuel 17. Each time I read the story, I am blessed with valuable life lessons. During one such reading, I was reminded of the lines that were drawn in the projects. In the story, Goliath and the Philistines represent one side. David and the army of

Israel represent the other. The valley of Elah represents *the line* that stood between them. In verse 8, the giant Goliath is shouting threats from a distance, from the other side of the line. Every time he would shout, the army of Israel would tremble with fear. That was the army's first mistake. Since Goliath was allowed to get away with that, he continued to move closer to Israel's camp. In verse 25, you see him crossing the valley, strutting into Israel's camp with his demoralizing threats.

We can learn a valuable lesson from our biblical predecessors. Instead of running in fear, Israel should have drawn the line and confronted the giant. Likewise, the giants in our lives should not be feared, they have to be faced; they cannot be denied, they have to be defeated.

Giants are not merely characters from ancient history. Twenty-first century giants can often be seen in our lives. They are our colossal challenges and seemingly impossible situations. They usually send us running in fear or keep us tossing and turning at night. Their thunderous threats consistently seek to drown out and ultimately destroy our hopes and dreams.

Our enemy, satan, deceitfully and deliberately positions giants right at the borders of our blessings and breakthroughs. We cannot afford to retreat in fear like the Israelites, forfeiting our promises and purposes. (Read Numbers 13-14.) Like David, we must confront, disarm, and behead our giants, rendering them powerless in our lives.

In the next few pages, I will share biblical principles and strategies (gleaned from Deuteronomy 1:19-34 and 1 Samuel 17) that I have used to destroy giants in my own life. Whether you are facing financial giants, giants on your job, giants in your home, or giants in your mind, these principles and strategies will transform you from victim to victor.

SEVEN WAYS TO SLAY A GIANT

1. *Dress for Success.* Most of the giants in our lives are not physical; they are spiritual. Our battles are not our addictions, afflictions, or associations – our spouses, our bosses, or our neighbors. Giants present themselves under these guises, but our battles are actually with the unseen demonic spirits that are sometimes working through these individuals (Ephesians 6:12).

MOST OF THE GIANTS IN OUR LIVES ARE NOT PHYSICAL; THEY ARE SPIRITUAL.

Studies show that less than sixty percent of Christians pray at least once a day, and an even smaller percentage read and study the Bible daily. It is no wonder that these startling statistics are true. Satan knows where our strength lies, and he understands that if he keeps us too busy and too distracted to develop these disciplines in our lives, then we are no threat to his kingdom.

An extremely effective marketing campaign instructs us to never leave home without their credit card. As a cardholder I can attest to the fact that it's nice to have this sense of security. Whether I am dining, traveling, shopping, doing business, or just going about my daily activities, with my card, I am prepared to handle expected and unexpected financial transactions. As Christians, we know that we are engaged in a constant spiritual battle. Though our position in Christ guarantees us the victory, we must be dressed for the enemy's futile attacks at all times (Ephesians 6:10-17).

In 1 Samuel 17, David did not have to go home to get his slingshot or borrow Saul's armor for the battle. He was already equipped and familiar with a weapon (his slingshot) that had been tested and proven effective. We can learn a valuable lesson here. We cannot depend on our parents, our pastors, or any other person for our weaponry and defense. We have to suit up for ourselves. Do not be caught off guard. "Be careful! Watch out for attacks from

126

the devil, your great enemy. He prowls around like a roaring lion, looking for some victim to devour" (1 Peter 5:8).

2. *Stay focused.* Along the journey to peace, purpose, and abundant living, we will encounter many distractions. The only way to ensure safe travel and successful arrivals is to journey by faith, seeking and following divine directions. Journeying by faith does not mean stumbling blindly. When we seek God's guidance through prayer and His Word, He will instruct us in the ways that we should go (Psalm 32:8). Our responsibility is to stay focused and to direct our attention to Him, not to our circumstances.

In Numbers 13-14, the Lord had given the Israelites a promise concerning the land of Canaan. It was bountiful, and it was theirs. Though all twelve of the spies sent to explore the land witnessed its bounty, ten of them lost sight of the promise in the face of the problem: giants.

> MANY OF US HAVE RECEIVED MAGNIFICENT VISIONS, DREAMS, AND PROMISES FROM THE LORD, BUT WE HAVE ALLOWED OUR CIRCUMSTANCES TO KEEP US FROM POSSESSING THEM.

Many of us have received magnificent visions, dreams, and promises from the Lord, but we have allowed our circumstances to keep us from possessing them. The Israelites were faced with a destiny-determining question, and so are we. Are we going to believe God and His promises, or are we going to believe our circumstances? Belief in this case does not deny reality, but rather denotes trust or confidence. The giants in the land of Canaan were real, and so are our circumstances. Our challenge is to never elevate our circumstances above God's promises. Our trust and confidence should be in God and His Word. If He said it, we should believe it.

Only two of the twelve spies, Joshua and Caleb, believed God. They *saw* the giants but *stayed focused* on the promise. They believed that God would allow them to conquer the giants and possess the land (Numbers 14:6-9). David faced Goliath, but *stayed focused* on the Lord Almighty (1 Samuel 17:45-47).

You may be on the verge of God's promise to you today, as you face seemingly insurmountable giants. Don't give up. Stay focused on the promise. You may see unemployment – *stay focused* on His promise of provision. You may see cancer – *stay focused* on His promise of healing. You may see slanderous attacks – *stay focused* on His promise of protection. You may see "lack" – *stay focused* on His promise of "abundance." You may see addiction and defeat – *stay focused* on His promises of deliverance and victory.

As believers, we walk by faith, not by sight (2 Corinthians 5:7). In spite of what we see, we must continuously direct our attention to His promises.

3. Choose your battles wisely. Not every conflict needs to result in combat. Some battles are just not worth the cost. I've had to learn this lesson the hard way.

Living in the projects and in a household with five older brothers (one of whom I'll call Goliath, Jr.) required me to become a "fighter" at a very early age. Fighting was something that in most cases I had to do whether I wanted to or not. It was necessary for survival. I never went looking for fights, but somehow they managed to find me (often in hiding).

I am grateful for the godly determination, perseverance, and courage that are characteristic of the "fighter" in me. The Lord has used these traits to lead me victoriously through situations where throwing in the towel would have been much easier. For instance, it's good to be a fighter when sickness and disease are waging war in your body. It is good to be a fighter when the enemy is after your marriage, your child, or your mind.

I am equally grateful that God has revealed to me the destructive side of this fighting spirit. Thankfully, the physical fights ended in my youth, but not without an internal struggle. I am ashamed to admit how often I have wanted to jump over the counter onto a rude sales clerk, pull a discourteous driver out of the car onto the concrete, or knock the wind out of a condescending colleague. Sounds crazy, doesn't it? It is. These types of battles are not worth fighting, but unfortunately, I entertained far too many before heeding the Lord's firm and loving rebuke. Again, no more physical fights, but I became quite adept at pulverizing with my tongue or retaliating in some other "wouldn't-want-any-of-my-church-friends-to-see-me" way. I had to learn to choose my battles wisely.

In selecting a successor for Moses, God chose Joshua, the brilliant military strategist who eventually led the Israelites victoriously into Canaan.

> Then Moses said to the Lord, "O Lord, the God of the spirits of all living things, please appoint a new leader for the community. Give them someone who will lead them into battle, so the people of the Lord will not be like sheep without a shepherd."
>
> The Lord replied, "Take Joshua son of Nun, who has the Spirit in him, and lay your hands on him. Present him to Eleazar the priest before the whole community, and publicly commission him with the responsibility of leading the people."
>
> NUMBERS 27:15-19

In this passage, the Lord highlights the crucial criteria for the leader He would use to fulfill His promise to the Israelites: Joshua had the Spirit in him. The Lord further voices His approval of Joshua by highlighting the fact that Joshua sought His guidance when direction was needed (Numbers 27:21). This is a power-packed passage with a simple but profound message: *Let the Lord choose your battles!*

God wants to lead and guide us by His Spirit. We tend to pick our battles and then ask God for strength, but He may want to instruct us as He did Joshua in the victory at Jericho (Joshua 6): "Seek Me...follow My instructions, and you won't even have to fight. The battle has already been won!" (author's paraphrase).

> THERE ARE VERY FEW PAINS AS EXCRUCIATING AS THAT OF BETRAYAL, AND IT IS EVEN MORE INTENSIFIED WHEN THE WOUNDS ARE INFLICTED BY THOSE CLOSE TO YOU.

One of the most painful experiences of my life turned out to be a great opportunity for God to teach me this lesson in godly restraint. To summarize a very long and complex story, I was lied on, talked about, and mistreated by a group of people in whom I trusted and had invested a great deal personally and professionally. There are very few pains as excruciating as that of betrayal, and it is even more intensified when the wounds are inflicted by those close to you. Not only was I fiercely betrayed, but I never saw it coming. What a blow!

Suddenly, I found myself backed into a corner by insults, injuries, and injustices. Instead of seeking God and His guidance, my self-preservation instinct erupted from the corner, ready for a fight. My first thought was to defend myself. I spent many sleepless nights and exhausting days pleading my innocence, arguing with my assailants, and unsuccessfully rallying my *so-called* advocates.

I will never forget the night that I cried myself to sleep, pleading with God for protection from my enemies. The words He spoke to me are still piercing to this day. He asked me a direct question: "Are you going to be a victim or a victor?" "What do you mean?" I thought. "I'm doing the best I can." At this point, I realized I had been fighting a battle that I could not win. I needed God's guidance, strength, and power. The battle was not mine; it was the Lord's.

From that day forward, I sought God's guidance and carefully followed His directions. A different type of "fighter" was birthed in me. I began to study and meditate on God's Word, boldly confessing and believing for His promises of peace, protection, and provision. My focus switched from my enemies to my Shepherd (Psalm 23). God not only changed my perspective; He also did a whole new work in me. What the enemy meant for evil, God used for my good (Genesis 50:20).

I now realize God allowed that situation in my life to draw me closer to Him and to prepare me for the next phase of His purpose and plan for my life. New doors and opportunities opened for me that I would have otherwise overlooked. God returned everything that I had to walk away from to me – a hundredfold.

4. *Don't forget past victories.* A stanza of one of my favorite praise songs goes like this: *"Jesus, I'll never forget what you've done for me. Jesus, I'll never forget how you set me free. Jesus, I'll never forget how you brought me out. Jesus, I'll never forget...no, never."* Just writing the words makes me want to jump to my feet and dance all over the room. I don't know about you, but God has been good to me. He has brought me out of some serious situations.

The song goes on to say, *"How could I forget what He's done for me. How could I forget how he set me free...?"* This is a very good

CONFESSIONS OF A KEPT WOMAN

question. How could we forget the many acts of kindness that God has performed in each of our lives and those He continues to perform on a daily basis? The enemy certainly wants us to forget. He wants us to become so paralyzed by our current "battles" that we forget about our past and present blessings.

In Numbers 13:27-29, the Israelites were so paralyzed by fear of the giants that lay ahead that they quickly forgot about the brutal bondage from which the Lord had delivered them back in Egypt. Not only had God delivered them from the bonds of slavery, but He had also protected and provided for them in the wilderness. God had proven himself faithful, but forgetting His proven character, the Israelites shrank back with fear in the face of their circumstances.

On the other hand, David "never forgot" what the Lord did for him (1 Samuel 17:34-37). He exclaims in the face of the giants and the doubters, "The Lord who saved me from the claws of the lion and the bear will save me from this Philistine!" David learned to rely on the Lord's faithfulness. God had done it before, and David trusted Him to do it again.

Take a moment to think about all that God has done for you. You do not have to go back very far; simply start listing the things that He has done for you today. In case you may need some help, He allowed you to see this day. Thousands of people around the world died in their sleep; expired on hospital ventilators; or had their lives extinguished at the hands of gunmen, by drunk drivers, or in some other sudden manner. But you made it. Not only did you make it, but you got up this morning and got dressed. (You may not be clad in designer originals or haute couture, but you're dressed.) The fact that you are reading this book and understanding the subject matter tells me that you are in your right mind. Furthermore, the fact that this book has not been translated in Braille lets me know that you have sight. These blessings alone are enough to shout about. Do you need more examples? Get in your car (another blessing) and drive to the closest hospital. Take a walk (another blessing) through the emergency room and then visit a few floors, particularly the critical and intensive care units. I hope you're getting the point – we have so much for which to be thankful.

Whenever I feel the spirit of heaviness falling on me, weighing me down with my "wants," I immediately begin to thank God for what I already have. The heaviness always lifts from me when I do this, and I encourage you to do the same. Consider the contrasting actions of David and the Israelites. Both were faced with seemingly impossible situations. Both had witnessed God's goodness at various times in their lives. Both stood at the brinks of God's promises in their lives. The Israelites forgot and regressed. David remembered and progressed.

> WHATEVER GOD HAS STARTED IN YOU, HE WILL COMPLETE.

You may be facing some giants in your own life, but do not forget. Do not forget that God gave you the job that you have, so He can give you another one or your own business! Do not forget that God gave you the house in which you live, and He can surely provide the mortgage payments.

Whatever God has started in you, He will complete.

> And I am convinced and sure of this very thing,
> that He Who began a good work in you will continue
> until the day of Jesus Christ [right up to the time
> of His return], developing [that good work] and
> perfecting and bringing it to full completion in you.
> PHILIPPIANS 1:6 (AMP)

But watch out! Be very careful never to forget what you
have seen the Lord do for you. Do not let these things
escape your mind as long as you live! And be sure to pass
them on to your children and grandchildren

DEUTERONOMY 4:9

5. *Step out from the "crowd."* If you are ever going to accomplish
anything great for God, you are going to have to step out from the
crowd. You must be willing to ignore popular opinion and follow
divine directions. Too often in life, we allow others' opinions to
determine our actions. I wonder how many dreams have been
shattered because popular opinion could not imagine them. How
many visions have been abandoned because popular opinion could
not see them? If we wait to receive the "green light" of popular
opinion before moving forward on any plan, dream, or assignment,
we will never pass the starting line.

There will always be those who think you
cannot, should not, or will not. However, once you
have received directions from the Lord, whose
opinion matters most, you must move forward
by faith. The Israelites allowed popular opinion
to keep them from entering the Promised Land.

OTHERS CANNOT
ALWAYS SEE
WHAT GOD HAS
SHOWN YOU.

Only Joshua and Caleb, the two who believed God, were allowed
to enter. David's decision to face Goliath was met with a great deal
of ridicule and criticism, but he did not allow this to dissuade him.
He moved forward in God-confidence and defeated the giant.

Others cannot always see what God has shown you. Sometimes,
it is even difficult for you to see it in the natural, but you have to see
it by faith. I remember thinking when I started my own consulting
business several years ago, "Lord, this is hard." And it was. It was
much harder to believe God for contracts than it was to receive a

paycheck on the 15th and 30th of each month. It was much harder to be the CEO, accountant, secretary, and maid than it was to have a staff performing assigned duties. God's reply to me that day has become my motivation in every challenging endeavor. He simply said, "Barbara, if entrepreneurship were easy, everybody would have their own business." You can fill in the blanks with your own challenges. If (blank) were easy, everybody would (blank). If marriages were easy, everybody would have healthy, happy ones. If dieting and exercise were easy, everybody would be physically fit.

No matter what the decision may be in life, there will always be an array of opinions. We must be prayerful and careful about the ones that we allow to influence us.

> But my child, be warned:
> There is no end of opinions ready to be expressed.
> Studying them can go on
> forever and become very exhausting!
> Here is my final conclusion:
> Fear God and obey his commands,
> for this is the duty of every person.
> ECCLESIASTES 12:12-13

People tend to offer advice derived from their own experiences, fears, and limitations. In most cases, they mean well but are still unable to objectively instruct us. Knowing this, we would be wise to adhere to the advice of Christian author and speaker Joyce Meyer: "Run to the throne instead of the phone." I am not saying – and neither do I believe is Joyce – that wise counsel should be ignored. I thank God for good Christian friends and confidantes, but even they sometimes cannot see the whole picture.

Furthermore, not everyone can handle the revelation that God has given you. Be careful and ask God to show you when and in whom to confide. Others' lack of faith (not to mention jealousy and envy) can weaken your resolve, causing you to surrender right at the brink of your victory.

Extraordinary deeds require extraordinary faith, out-of-the-box thinking, and uncommon courage. We must learn to trust God as the final authority in all of our decisions. After all, He is omniscient. He sees and knows that which man cannot fully comprehend.

"My thoughts are completely different from yours,"
says the Lord. "And my ways are far beyond
anything you could imagine.
For just as the heavens are higher than the earth,
so are my ways higher than your ways and
my thoughts higher than your thoughts."

ISAIAH 55:8-9

6. *Believe you can.* Believing is the foundation of achieving. In Mark 9:23, Jesus proclaims, "Anything is possible if a person believes." Many of us journey through life with "can't complexes." We never experience the thrill of victory because our minds are programmed for defeat. We think defeated thoughts and live defeated lives. Victory begins in our minds. We must believe that we "can."

GOD WILL NEVER "CALL" YOU TO DO SOMETHING WITHOUT GIVING YOU EVERYTHING YOU NEED TO COMPLETE THE ASSIGNMENT.

God will never "call" you to do something without giving you everything you need to complete the assignment. Paul tells us in Philippians 4:13 that we can do all things through Christ who strengthens us. Joshua and Caleb understood this (Numbers 14:6-9). They knew that God was with them and believed that they could conquer the land and its inhabitants. David understood this (1 Samuel 17:45-47). He knew that with the Lord

Almighty, he could conquer Goliath.

Whenever we decide to step out and walk by faith, there will likely be "giants" positioned along the path to oppose, frighten, and discourage us. We must keep the faith, trusting and believing that greater is the Holy Spirit who lives in us than the spirit who lives in the world (1 John 4:4). We must believe that we have the power within us to conquer the giants and claim God's promises.

The following poem clearly and concisely illustrates this principle:

You Can

If you think you're beaten, you are;
If you think you dare not, you don't;
If you like to win but think you can't,
It's almost a cinch you won't.
If you think you're outclassed you are,
Because you've got to think high to rise.
You've got to be sure of yourself before
you can ever win a prize.
Life's battles don't always go to
the strongest or fastest man,
but sooner or later the one who wins
is the one who thinks he can.

— AUTHOR UNKNOWN –

7. *Give God the glory.* The final and most important step in the giant-slaying strategy is to give God the glory. Though we must believe that we can conquer the giants in our lives, we must never forget that it is by God's grace and strength that we are allowed to triumph in these situations. We must acknowledge His presence and His power in every phase of the victory. David's final words

to Goliath before the fatal blow were, "And everyone will know that the Lord does not need weapons to rescue His people. It is His battle, not ours. The Lord will give you to us" (1 Samuel 17:47). David had no intentions of claiming the Lord's victory as his own.

Too often, we step into the Lord's limelight, claiming for ourselves the glory that belongs solely to Him. No matter how hard you worked or what you sacrificed, it was God who allowed you to accomplish that feat about which you now boast. How could you have worked hard without the health and strength that he provided? What could you have sacrificed – including time, talent, and resources – that He did not provide?

Isaiah asks a very poignant question in Isaiah 10:15: "Can an ax boast greater power than the person who uses it?" You and I are only as effective and as powerful as God allows us to be. We are simply the tools He uses to do great works. Therefore, we would be wise to heed Paul's instructions first quoted in 1 Corinthians 1:32 and again in 2 Corinthians 10:17:

> As the Scriptures say,
> "The person who wishes to boast
> should boast only of what the Lord has done."

We must declare like the psalmist,

> Not to us, O Lord, but to you goes all the
> glory for your unfailing love and faithfulness.
>
> PSALM 115:1

THOUGHT QUESTIONS

1. Are you facing any giants today – people or situations that have held you hostage to fear? Who or what are they? Determine today that you will not allow them to destroy your hopes and dreams.

_____

_____

_____

_____

_____

_____

_____

2. Which pieces, if any, of God's armor are you not using on a daily basis? How might this exposure leave you vulnerable to the enemy's attacks against you?

_____

_____

_____

_____

_____

3. What has God done for you lately (within the last few days)?
Take some time to write out a prayer of thanksgiving.

_____

_____

_____

_____

_____

_____

_____

_____

_____

_____

4. If fear was not a factor, which dreams or visions would you
pursue at this time in your life?

_____

_____

_____

_____

_____

_____

_____

_____

5. Has God given you a big and seemingly impossible vision or goal? If yes, good! These are the ones that give Him the greatest glory. Write a faith confession regarding this vision. Include "I can!" statements. For example: *God has given me the wisdom, insight, and gifts that I need to speak into the lives of others through "Confessions of a Kept Woman." I can complete and publish this book. I have the strength, support, and financial resources that I need. Favor surrounds me like a shield. God will provide countless opportunities for this book to be a blessing in the lives of others.*

_____

_____

_____

_____

_____

_____

_____

_____
_____
_____
_____
_____
_____
_____

6. What did God reveal to you through this chapter?

_____
_____
_____
_____
_____
_____
_____
_____
_____
_____
_____
_____

_____

_____

_____

_____

_____

_____

_____

_____

_____

What will you do with these revelations? Which changes will you make? Which actions will you take?

_____

_____

_____

_____

_____

_____

_____

_____

CONFESSIONS

I am strong in the Lord and in the power of His might. I am dressed in the whole armor of God that protects me from the attacks of the enemy. Though I may be in the midst of a battle, I am confident of the victory in Christ Jesus.
(Ephesians 6:10-17)

God is always with me. I constantly meditate on, speak, and obey His Word. I enjoy good success in every area of my life, and not one of my enemies is able to stand against me.
(Joshua 1:5-8)

God gives me the strength that I need in every situation. With Him, I am able to accomplish anything.
(Philippians 4:13)

I do not allow fear and intimidation to prevent me from receiving God's promises. In every situation, I magnify God, not my problems. Though the "giants" in my life may appear to be undefeatable, I am well able to conquer them.
(Numbers 13:30-33, 14:6-9)

Lord, I thank You with all of my heart. I worship and praise You for Your love and Your faithfulness. You always fulfill Your promises. When I pray, You answer me, giving me the courage and the strength that I need.
(Psalm 138:1-3)

Lord, You've done so much for me. I can't keep quiet about Your goodness. For the rest of my life, I'll sing praises to You. I'm eternally grateful to you, Lord.
(Psalm 30:12)

Which point from this chapter speaks directly to one of your personal situations? Search God's Word for relevant promises and write a faith confession concerning the matter.

_____

_____

_____

_____

_____

_____

May the Lord bless you and keep you.

May He smile on you and be gracious to you.

May He surround you with His favor and

give you His perfect peace.

– NUMBERS 6:24–26 –

NOTES

CHAPTER 1

1. *Merriam Webster's Collegiate Dictionary, Tenth Edition,* 1995.
2. Ibid.

CHAPTER 2

1. Rick Renner, *Sparkling Gems from the Greek* (Tulsa, OK: Teach All Nations, 2003), 314.

CHAPTER 3

1. Rick Warren, *The Purpose Driven Life* (Grand Rapids, MI: Zondervan, 2002), 17-18.

CHAPTER 4

1. *Merriam Webster's Collegiate Dictionary, Tenth Edition,* 1995.
2. Ibid.

CHAPTER 5

1. *Merriam Webster's Collegiate Dictionary, Tenth Edition,* 1995.

ABOUT THE AUTHOR

Barbara Harris Curtis is a gifted writer, speaker, and minister of the Gospel. She is committed to motivating and inspiring individuals to find purpose and passion in both their personal and professional lives. This commitment and the belief that we are "blessed to be a blessing" are the impetus behind her mission to serve humankind. She currently serves in full-time ministry at Lakewood Church in Houston, Texas.

In 1999, a vision from God and a desire to take biblically-based training into corporate and non-profit arenas led Barbara to establish RSVP – Realize Success through Vision and Purpose, a consulting and training company. Through conferences, seminars, and public speaking engagements, she shares her ministry experience and empowering messages with individuals, churches, and other organizations throughout the country.

Barbara and her husband Larry reside in Houston, Texas.

You may contact Barbara Harris Curtis at:
Back2Back Books
P.O. Box 22651
Houston, Texas 77227-2651
Email: back2back@houston.rr.com